Homework, Organization, and Planning Skills (HOPS) Interventions

Homework, Organization, and Planning Skills (HOPS) Interventions

By Joshua M. Langberg, PhD

A TREATMENT MANUAL

From the NASP Publications Board Operations Manual
The content of this document reflects the ideas and positions of the authors. The responsibility lies solely with the authors and does not necessarily reflect the position or ideas of the National Association of School Psychologists.

Published by the National Association of School Psychologists

Copies may be ordered from:
NASP Publications
4340 East West Highway, Suite 402
Bethesda, MD 20814
(301) 657-0270
(301) 657-0275, fax
(866) 331-NASP, Toll Free
e-mail: *publications@naspweb.org*
www.nasponline.org

ISBN 978-0-932955-62-3

Printed in the United States of America

16   10 9 8 7 6 5 4 3

Dedication

To my family, Lisa, Kaitlin, and Alexis,
whose love and support energize and inspire my work.

Table of Contents

SUPPLEMENTAL CD-ROM

- Evening Schedule
- Homework Assignment Tracking Sheet
- Materials Organization Plan
- Missing Assignments Tracking Plan
- Organizational Skills Checklist
- Parent Checklist
- Parent Checklist Plan
- Points System Tracking Sheet
- Progress Tracking Sheet
- Rewards Menu
- Self-Management Checklist
- Self-Management Plan
- Teacher Initials Checklist
- Teacher Introduction Letter
- Teacher Update Letter 1
- Teacher Update Letter 2
- Time Management Checklist

Preface

This Homework, Organization, and Planning Skills (HOPS) intervention was developed through a systematic process of collaboration with school psychologists and school counselors (referred to as school mental health [SMH] providers). SMH providers implemented the HOPS intervention and provided feedback designed to make the manual user friendly and feasible to implement in the school setting during the school day. As a result, the HOPS intervention is structured to be delivered through a series of 16 brief sessions (20 minutes or less) with an SMH provider and student. However, the interventions presented in this manual are also appropriate for use by clinical psychologists, social workers, and counselors who work in clinical settings. For that reason, we use clinician throughout the manual as a general term that includes SMH providers. Portions of the intervention could also be implemented by teachers. Information on how to adapt the HOPS intervention for clinic settings and for implementation by teachers can be found in chapter 2, "Practical Applications and Adaptations."

The HOPS intervention was developed specifically for children of middle school age with attention problems or with a diagnosis of attention deficit hyperactivity disorder (ADHD). This focus is because children with ADHD frequently experience increased difficulties with organization and planning following the transition to middle school that result in academic failure. However, the skills the HOPS intervention teaches are necessary for academic success, irrespective of a child's diagnosis, attentional issues, or grade in school. Our earlier research demonstrated that students generally classified as at risk—meaning that they were struggling with organization and planning but did not necessarily meet criteria for ADHD—also benefited from these types of interventions. Further, the HOPS intervention has been effectively implemented with elementary-age children in the third and fourth grades, and certain components (e.g., time management) would be appropriate for use with high school students. The HOPS intervention in its entirety—that is, delivering all interventions in order—is appropriate for any student with difficulties with organization and planning in grades 3 through 10.

The HOPS intervention was designed to fit well with the response-to-intervention (RTI) framework being implemented in many schools in the United States. Consistent with an RTI approach, the HOPS intervention is a research-based program that uses frequent assessment and monitoring to gauge students' progress and the need for supplemental intervention. The HOPS intervention is structured so that organizational skills are introduced first, homework management skills are introduced next, and time management and planning skills are introduced last. However, mastery of the early skills is not necessarily a prerequisite for introduction of the later skills. As suggested in an RTI approach, functional assessment should drive decisions about which skills to teach and in what order.

Implemented exactly as outlined in this book, the HOPS program would be considered a Tier 3 intervention because it targets children with attention problems and is implemented on an individual basis (student–teacher ratio of 1:1). The HOPS program can also be adapted to serve as a Tier 2 intervention to reach larger groups of children, such as children considered at risk for academic problems. In chapter 2, we discuss adaptations that allow the HOPS protocol to be delivered as a Tier 2 intervention—for example, as a group-based program rather than on an individual basis.

This manual divides each intervention session into two parts: (a) presession reading for the clinician, and (b) the actual session content. We encourage clinicians to make time to review the presession reading prior to implementing each intervention session. We also suggest that clinicians read the entire book before implementing the intervention to get an overview of the program. Feedback from the SMH providers who assisted with this manual's development suggests that a fair amount of presession planning is required the first time the intervention is implemented with a student. Clinicians should be prepared to devote 20 minutes of preparation time per session for at least the first few HOPS intervention sessions. SMH providers who have implemented the HOPS program suggest that it is considerably easier the second time through and requires significantly less preparation effort.

Acknowledgments

First and foremost, I would like to acknowledge the importance of Dr. Steven Evans's work with adolescents with attention deficit hyperactivity disorder (ADHD) as the basis for the interventions presented in this book. Dr. Evans developed the Challenging Horizons Program (CHP), a school-based intervention for adolescents with ADHD. Many of the interventions described in this book are adaptations of CHP interventions. I would also like to thank the National Association of School Psychologists (NASP) publication staff for their helpful feedback in making this treatment manual user friendly. In particular, I would like to thank Dr. Thomas Power for his input. I am especially grateful to all of the school mental health providers who volunteered their time and effort to help develop and refine the interventions in this book. They implemented the HOPS interventions and provided feedback because they are devoted to improving the academic performance of children with problems with organizational and planning skills. Finally, I would like to thank those individuals who contributed to the book by reading drafts and providing feedback: Dr. Jeff Epstein, Dr. Aaron Vaughn, Dr. Erin Girio, Lauren Rockwell, and Hillary Culp.

Funding to develop and refine the HOPS intervention was provided by grant R305A090305 awarded to Cincinnati Children's Hospital Medical Center from the U.S. Department of Education, Institute for Education Sciences. The views expressed are solely those of the author and do not necessarily represent the views or policy of the U.S. Department of Education.

Chapter 1

Importance of Organization and Planning Skills: Development of the HOPS Intervention

ORGANIZATION AND PLANNING SKILLS AS A PART OF CHILD DEVELOPMENT

Organization, planning, and time management skills are important aspects of successful functioning at home, school, and work. Students who have even minor difficulties with these skills, particularly in the school setting, can experience significant functional impairment. In schools, four academic activities are largely responsible for determining students' grades: classwork, homework, tests, and projects. A student's ability to organize and plan is central to each of these activities. Classwork requires that students work efficiently and manage their time well. To be successful with homework, students must maintain an organizational system that helps them accurately record assignments and transfer materials to and from school. To perform well on tests and long-term projects, students must be able to break tasks down into small, manageable steps and to plan ahead for the completion of each step.

Students who struggle with these skills are more likely than their peers to fail to bring home assignments, not know what was assigned, procrastinate when completing homework assignments, fail to complete homework, and forget to bring assignments back to class (Langberg, Arnold, et al., 2010; Power, Werba, Watkins, Angelucci, & Eiraldi, 2006). In addition, these children often have disorganized school binders, bookbags, lockers, and desks and, as a result, lose and cannot find materials (Langberg, Epstein, Urbanowicz, et al., 2008; Zentall, Harper, & Stormont-Spurgin, 1993). These difficulties can prevent children from reaching their full academic potential.

The importance of organizational and planning skills does not diminish over time. In fact, mastery of these skills becomes even more crucial as students progress through secondary school. Further, these skills remain important in the college setting (Blase et al., 2009; Norwalk, Norvilits, & MacLean, 2009; Reaser, Prevatt, Petscher, & Proctor, 2007) and are key ingredients for successful occupational functioning (Barkley, Murphy, & Fischer, 2008; Safren et al., 2005).

Children who struggle with organization, planning, and time management often begin to experience academic impairment early in elementary school. Expectations for time management and planning are typically minimal from kindergarten through the third grade. As a result, difficulties with materials organization are often evident prior to problems with time management and planning. In early elementary school, problems with organizational skills manifest as messy and disorganized desks and bookbags. These students will also have difficulty transferring materials to and from school without misplacing items. Fortunately, levels of parent and teacher support and monitoring are high during this period, and children are sometimes able to succeed academically despite difficulties with organization.

As children progress toward adolescence, parent and teacher support tend to diminish, and children are expected to function more autonomously. At the same time that parents and teachers are encouraging autonomy, environmental demands and responsibilities are increasing. In the school setting, academic demands increase significantly as children progress toward middle school. Children receive more homework, and schools are putting increased emphasis on tests and long-term projects, tasks that require time management and planning. Parents and teachers become less willing to provide reminders or prompts or to monitor homework and test preparation behaviors. Many children experience a tipping point around the transition to middle school, when the reduced supports and increased academic demands combine with the student's use of ineffective organization and time management strategies and result in academic failure.

Middle School Environment

The transition to middle school is frequently a difficult period for students with organization and planning difficulties (Langberg, Epstein, Altaye, et al., 2008). The environmental changes that occur with the transition to middle school are more abrupt and substantial than at any other time in a student's educational development, with the possible exception of the transition to college. Children often go from having one or two teachers to having three to five separate teachers. Children are required to manage a different set of materials for each class and must make the transition between classes during the school day. Academic demands increase rapidly; students must manage homework, tests, and projects for three or four different core class subjects—reading, math, social studies, and science.

Teachers too have a different experience. In elementary school, teachers are responsible for one or two classrooms and spend between half day and a full day with the same group of students. This schedule allows teachers to closely monitor and supervise students' behavior. By contrast, in the middle school setting, teachers interact with each child for between 1 and 2 hours per day and are responsible for upward of 60 children. Accordingly, teachers are unable to offer the close monitoring and oversight that students may have received during elementary school. For example, in elementary school, a teacher might support a child with organizational problems by ensuring that the child has the necessary materials in his or her bookbag at the end of the school day. This type of individual intervention is no longer feasible in the middle school environment.

Children's relationships with their parents are also changing rapidly during this period of development. Parents often struggle with the balance between "doing everything for my child" and "doing nothing." Parents frequently feel that their children should be managing school materials on their own and are no longer willing to provide consistent monitoring and support, for example, checking their child's bookbag every morning before school and checking with teachers about homework assignments every day after school. Parents often feel conflicted between wanting to promote autonomous behavior and the realization that if they stop assisting with academics their child may fail. Further, young adolescents want to be trusted and viewed as responsible. When parents choose to closely monitor academic behaviors, such as by checking with the teacher about the accuracy of homework recording, adolescents often feel that they are being treated unfairly and may respond with noncompliant or disrespectful behaviors. Accordingly, parent–child conflict over organization and planning often increases during this period.

Children With Attention Deficit Hyperactivity Disorder

One group of children that frequently exhibits difficulties with organization and time management in the school setting is children with attention deficit hyperactivity disorder (ADHD). ADHD is one of the most common behavioral disorders in children (Froehlich et al., 2007). Several of the primary diagnostic symptoms of ADHD relate specifically to problems with organization and planning—that is, the child often has difficulty organizing tasks and activities, often loses things, is often forgetful, and often fails to finish schoolwork, chores, or duties (American Psychiatric Association, 2000). Not surprisingly, academic impairment is one of the most prominent difficulties faced by children and adolescents with ADHD (DuPaul & Stoner, 2003). Children with ADHD are more likely than their peers to forget to bring materials from school to home and vice versa, to have homework assignments recorded inaccurately, to procrastinate when completing homework assignments, and to leave work incomplete (Langberg, Arnold, et al., 2010; Power et al., 2006). Children with ADHD often have disorganized desks, school binders, bookbags, and lockers, and as a result, frequently lose and cannot find homework materials (Abikoff & Gallagher, 2008a; Atkins, Pelham, & Licht, 1989; Langberg, Epstein, & Graham, 2008; Zentall et al., 1993). Further, when completing homework, children with ADHD often have difficulty staying on-task, rush through their assignments, and make careless mistakes (Epstein, Polloway, Foley, & Patton, 1993; Power, Karustis, & Habboushe, 2001). As a result, children and adolescents with ADHD earn significantly lower school grades than their non-ADHD peers (Frazier, Youngstrom, Glutting, & Watkins, 2007; Molina et al., 2009).

INTERVENTIONS THAT ADDRESS ORGANIZATION AND PLANNING SKILLS

Given that children with ADHD consistently display problems with organization and planning that interfere with their academic functioning, an intervention is needed that addresses these difficulties. Interventions have been developed that target problems with homework (Power, Karustis, & Habboushe, 2001) and with organization (Abikoff & Gallagher, 2008a; Evans, Serpell, Schultz, & Pastor, 2007; Pfiffner et al., 2007). However, none of these interventions were designed specifically for school mental health (SMH) providers to implement in the school setting during the school day. A treatment manual for implementing organizational and planning interventions directly in the school setting is needed because the school is where most of these difficulties occur. In addition, delivering interventions in the school setting can improve access to care and may also improve intervention outcomes and generalization of improvements (Evans, Langberg, & Williams, 2003). It is important to develop an intervention specifically for SMH providers because they are on the front lines when it comes to interventions for academic problems. They have the ability to identify problems early and to intervene before difficulties compound and lead to more severe negative academic outcomes such as school dropout. Further, SMH providers have daily access to students, which allows them to provide the frequent monitoring and contingency management that is necessary to improve organizational skills.

Development of the Homework, Organization, and Planning Skills (HOPS) Intervention

The first step in the development process was to select the core intervention components that would make up the HOPS intervention. The goal was to directly link each intervention component to a specific problem that is caused by organization and planning difficulties in the school setting. Figure 1 outlines the theoretical rationale for the HOPS intervention components and shows how each intervention component targets a specific area of impairment.

Once the core elements of the intervention were established, our team developed a specific set of procedures (a treatment manual) for implementing the intervention in a school setting. The next step was to evaluate the effects of the intervention on improving children's organization and planning skills and academic performance.

To accomplish this, we enrolled 37 students with ADHD (31 boys and 6 girls, ages 9–14) in an intervention study (Langberg, Epstein, Urbanowicz, Simon, & Graham, 2008). The students were randomly assigned to receive the intervention in the fall school semester or were put on a waiting list to receive the intervention later in the school year (a wait-list control group). Participants in the study attended grades 4 through 7 in a suburban public school district in southwest Ohio.

The intervention was delivered as part of an on-site after-school program that took place 2 days per week for 8 weeks. The after-school program was staffed by university undergraduate psychology students with a ratio of 3:1, after school program participants to counselors. All participants received 20 minutes of individual intervention time (1:1 student to counselor) each program day, during which time the organization and time management interventions were implemented. Participants were taught to develop and maintain systems of organizing school materials for school binders, bookbags, and lockers. Participants were also taught how to accurately record homework assignments and tests in a planner or assignment book and to plan for long-term projects and tests by breaking tasks into smaller, more manageable components. The counselors running the

FIGURE 1. Rationale for the HOPS intervention components.

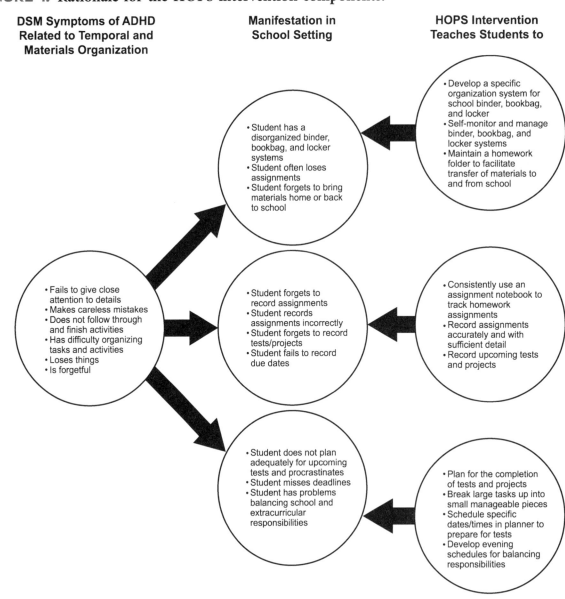

program completed checklists to track the students' progress with materials organization and homework management, and the students' parents completed a rating scale that assessed problems their child was having with homework management and completion. Students' grade point average (GPA) was also examined.

The percentage of materials organization criteria (e.g., no loose papers in bookbag) that students met was recorded at baseline, twice per week for the 8-week intervention, and again at an 8-week follow-up. At baseline (i.e., the start of the intervention), participants met 38% of binder criteria, 69% of bookbag criteria, and 47% of locker criteria. Students improved and were meeting 98%, 92%, and 95% of criteria, respectively, by the final program day. At the 8-week follow-up, students' organization had decreased slightly—72% binder, 81% bookbag, and 83% locker—but remained improved over baseline. At baseline, intervention group participants were writing down homework assignments and test dates in their planners 30% of the time. During the final 2 weeks of the intervention, participants were accurately recording homework assignments and tests for all core classes 72% of the time. During the 8-week postintervention period, participants continued to record homework and tests accurately an average of 65% of the time. In comparison, wait-list control participants accurately recorded homework assignments in their planners only 21% of the time.

Parents indicated that participants in the intervention group significantly improved their ability to manage and complete homework during the 8-week intervention, whereas the wait-list control group had no significant change. Analyses of students' GPA revealed a significant improvement in core class grades for those students who participated in the intervention, with the intervention group improving from a GPA of 2.37 at baseline to a GPA of 2.63 postintervention.

Refinement of the HOPS Intervention

Once our initial study was completed, the next step in the intervention development process was to modify and refine the treatment manual for implementation by SMH providers during the school day. We wanted to ensure that the manual could be implemented during the school day (as opposed to as an after-school program) and with fidelity by school counselors and school psychologists (as opposed to research staff). Funding from the U.S. Department of Education, Institute for Education Sciences, was used to accomplish this goal.

Copies of the intervention manual were distributed to 10 SMH providers. Four of the SMH providers served an urban district, three a suburban district, and three a rural district. Each SMH provider reviewed the manual, implemented the intervention with one middle school student with ADHD, and participated in focus groups. The SMH providers implemented the HOPS intervention sessions, either before school or during the school day, using only the manual, that is, without consultation with research staff. The 10 adolescents who received the intervention made significant improvements in homework management and completion problems and organizational skills according to parent ratings completed pre- and postintervention (Langberg, Culp, Epstein, et al., 2010). In addition, parents reported high levels of satisfaction with the HOPS intervention. SMH providers' focus group feedback led to a number of important modifications to the HOPS program to ensure that the manual was user friendly and that the intervention could be implemented during the school day. For example, SMH providers provided important guidance regarding the level of parental involvement that was feasible.

Chapter 2

Overview of the HOPS Intervention: Practical Applications and Adaptations

OVERVIEW OF THE HOPS INTERVENTION

The HOPS intervention is designed to be delivered through a series of frequent but brief sessions with the clinician and student. The intervention is delivered in 16 sessions, with each session lasting no more than 20 minutes. All HOPS sessions in this manual are presented in two parts: presession reading and session content. The presession reading is designed to orient the clinician to the content that he or she will be delivering during the corresponding HOPS intervention session. The presession reading is not shared with the student.

Three main skill areas are covered as part of the HOPS program: school materials organization, homework management, and time management and planning. For materials organization, the clinician teaches the student a specific system for organizing his or her school binder, bookbag, and locker. The student is also taught an organization system for transferring homework materials to and from school. For homework management, the clinician teaches the student how to accurately and consistently record homework assignments, projects, and tests in a planner (sometimes referred to as an agenda or assignment book). In the time management and planning portion of the program, the clinician teaches the student to break up work on projects and studying for tests into small, manageable pieces, and to plan for the timely completion of each piece. The clinician also teaches the student a system for planning an evening schedule that balances extracurricular activities with school responsibilities. The first few HOPS sessions focus on materials organization and homework management; the middle sessions focus on time management and planning; and the final sessions focus on teaching students to self-monitor and maintain their systems (see the progress tracking sheet on the supplemental CD-ROM for an outline of session-by-session content).

HOPS Rewards System

The reward system is a critical component of the HOPS intervention. The system is designed to counter the fact that children with ADHD almost always choose to engage in the most immediately reinforcing behavior available (Barkley, 2006), even if doing so results in negative long-term consequences. For example, children with ADHD often fail to record homework assignments in their planners because not recording requires less effort and gets them out of class sooner (the immediate reinforcer). Similarly, children with ADHD may procrastinate when they are supposed to be completing work and studying for tests, because almost any other available activity—playing outside or playing video games—is more immediately reinforcing.

The goal of the HOPS reward system is to change behavior patterns by making rewards more immediately available when a student engages in productive organizing and planning behaviors. The HOPS intervention uses a point system to allow students to earn the rewards. The clinician completes checklists to evaluate the student's use of organization and homework management skills at every intervention session. Students receive points for each criterion they meet on these checklists (e.g., no loose papers in bookbag = 1 point). In later sessions, the clinician also completes an assessment of the student's use of time management skills, and the student earns points for planning for tests and projects. These points accumulate and the student trades in the points for gift cards or for other rewards (see Use of the HOPS Rewards System section). Giving students the opportunity to work toward a reward significantly increases the likelihood that they will choose to use the productive academic behaviors they have learned (e.g., keeping papers organized in a school binder).

Parent Meetings

The HOPS intervention also includes two parent meetings. The first meeting takes place early in the intervention and is designed to orient the parent to the program. The second meeting takes place near the completion of the intervention. The goal of the second parent meeting is to teach the parent how to take over the HOPS checklist completion and reward responsibilities from the clinician. Parents learn about the HOPS reward system and work with the clinician to establish a plan for providing home-based rewards (see HOPS parent involvement section for more detail).

PRACTICAL APPLICATIONS

The practical applications section covers a variety of topics that clinicians need to consider prior to implementing the HOPS intervention. This section describes the materials that clinicians will need to implement the HOPS intervention and rewards system and to track student progress. This section also describes practical aspects of introducing parents and teachers to the HOPS intervention and working with parents and teachers throughout the intervention's implementation.

Materials Needed to Implement the HOPS Intervention

All of the checklists and tracking sheets that the clinician needs to implement the HOPS intervention are provided on the supplemental CD-ROM. We recommend that clinicians establish a folder or small binder for each student they will be working with. The folder should be able to hold three-hole-punched papers. In the folder the clinician will need the following:

- HOPS Progress Tracking Sheet
- Organizational Skills Checklist
- Teacher Initials Checklist
- Time Management Checklist
- Points System Tracking Sheet
- Multiple copies of the Homework Assignment Recording Sheet
- Multiple copies of the Evening Schedule
- Materials Organization Plan Sheet

- Missing Assignments Tracking Plan
- Self-Management Checklist
- Self-Management Plan Sheet
- Graph paper for charting student's progress

HOPS Binder System Materials

In studies of the HOPS intervention (described in chapter 1), all student participants received a new binder, folders, dividers, paper, pens and pencils, and a pencil pouch during the second intervention session. Providing participants with these materials serves two purposes. First, receiving all new materials fosters students' interest in the program and increases their motivation to maintain the organization system. Second, the binder, in particular, can be expensive, and some families do not have the resources to purchase one. In the HOPS program, we recommend that students use a specific binder organization system, including the use of a 3-inch D-ring binder for managing all class materials. The HOPS program allows for flexibility in the binder system, and alternative options are described in the session 2 reading. If you are planning to use the specific binder system recommended in this manual you will need the following:

- One 3-inch D-ring binder
- Five or six folders that have inside pockets and come three-hole punched
- One packet of three-hole-punched dividers (typically, five or six per packet)
- One pencil and pen pouch that is three-hole punched
- One box of pens and one box of pencils
- One packet of loose-leaf paper

How to Track Student Progress With the HOPS Intervention

The HOPS intervention allows clinicians to be flexible with the pace that skills are introduced. This flexibility is important because the time the clinician spends doing troubleshooting varies considerably from student to student. Many students will progress quickly, and the clinician will be able to follow the HOPS session content exactly as outlined in the manual. Some students will make progress more slowly, and the clinician will need to spend extra sessions troubleshooting. When clinicians are implementing the HOPS intervention with multiple students, it can be difficult to keep track of the sessions and activities that have been completed and those that need to be completed. We recommend that clinicians print a HOPS progress tracking sheet (on the supplemental CD-ROM) for each student they are working with to keep track of progress in the intervention. The progress tracking form provides a space for clinicians to indicate which sessions have been completed and to make notes about specific activities that were covered or problem-solving strategies that were implemented.

Use of the HOPS Rewards System

The HOPS session content is written as if clinicians will be providing gift cards for the points that students earn. In practice, clinicians may not have the resources to use gift cards as rewards, and they can substitute alternative rewards using a rewards menu. The most effective rewards menus include a variety of reward options and point values (see "Example of a completed HOPS rewards menu form"). When choosing the possible rewards, the clinician should consider two key points. First, the rewards must be salient and meaningful to the child. Second, the child should be able to earn a reward frequently (at least every third week) in the program. Using the established HOPS points system (100 points = a reward) will ensure that the student earns rewards quickly enough to maintain motivation. This is important because long-term rewards are rarely effective for children with ADHD (e.g., a reward for improved report card grades).

In the HOPS intervention, students earn points for obtaining teacher initials to ensure that homework assignments are recorded accurately, maintaining a structured materials organization system, and planning for tests and projects. In the HOPS session content we specify how many points students earn for demonstrating each skill. For example, students earn 1 point for every teacher initial they receive. These point values are recommendations, and clinicians are encouraged to increase the point values associated with each skill as needed and to provide bonus points for achieving goals. For example, the clinician could provide 25 bonus points the first time a student receives teacher initials from all core class teachers (i.e., four expected and four received). This flexibility is particularly important early in the intervention process to engage the student in the intervention and motivate him or her to implement the skills. Ideally, a student would earn the first reward no later than the sixth HOPS intervention session.

Types of Students Who Can Benefit From the HOPS Intervention

HOPS was developed based on research and clinical experience demonstrating that students with ADHD have difficulties with organization, homework, and time management and that these difficulties are associated with academic underachievement. However, students do not need to meet criteria for ADHD to benefit from the HOPS intervention. For example, our earlier research demonstrated that students who were generally classified as "at risk," meaning that they were struggling academically but did not necessarily meet criteria for ADHD, also benefited from these types of interventions (Langberg et al., 2006).

Other students, such as children with a learning disorder (e.g., a reading disorder), have deficits in core skills such as reading, math, or writing that are not addressed with the HOPS intervention. Although students with a learning disorder may still benefit from the HOPS intervention, they will also require intensive direct instruction in their particular area of difficulty. Similarly, children who exhibit moderate to severe oppositional behaviors, such as noncompliance and arguing, may not benefit as much from the HOPS intervention compared with students without these behaviors. For example, a child diagnosed with oppositional defiant disorder (ODD) is likely to be resistant to establishing new organization and homework management systems, and progress with the intervention may be slow. Clinicians working with students with ODD may want to implement a contingency management system for the student's behavior during HOPS sessions. For example, the student could earn points during the session for complying with the clinician's requests and for actively participating. These points could be added to the points the student is earning for materials organization and homework management.

The HOPS intervention will be most effective when implemented with students whose academic problems are directly related to difficulties with organization and time management. A child who has low class grades primarily because he or she consistently loses work, fails to turn in assignments, and does not adequately prepare for tests would be an excellent candidate for the HOPS intervention. When working with a student who has multiple factors contributing to poor academic performance (e.g., problems with reading and materials organization difficulties), the clinician should not rely solely on the HOPS intervention. Instead, an appropriate range of services should be implemented, such as direct reading instruction along with HOPS intervention. Relying solely on the HOPS intervention when multiple factors are contributing to poor academic performance may cause students to become frustrated with their lack of overall academic progress (e.g., their school grades are not improving despite their significant efforts to improve their materials organization), ultimately decreasing their motivation to participate in the HOPS intervention.

SUPPLEMENT. Example of a completed HOPS Rewards Menu.

REWARDS MENU

Reward Options	Point Value
1. Pass to get out of homework	150
2. Pass to turn in homework 1 day late without penalty	100
3. Game time (e.g., play basketball) during a HOPS intervention session	150
4. Extra HOPS intervention session just to talk with the clinician (i.e., no HOPS work)	150
5. Extra HOPS session where student and clinician play games on the computer	150
6. Time with peers, such as permission to bring another student to a HOPS session to hang out	200
7.	

 Supplemental Materials: Blank copies of the forms and letters are provided on the CD. Permission is given for individual teachers, administrators, or other school personnel to reproduce any form labeled "Supplement."

Parent Involvement in HOPS

The HOPS intervention includes two meetings that the clinician, parent, and student all attend. The purpose of these meetings is to begin transferring the monitoring and reward responsibilities from the clinician to the parent. As a general rule, the more the parents are involved in the HOPS program, the better the outcomes will be. Further, parental involvement is important for ensuring that students continue to use the HOPS skills even after the clinician stops working with them.

Clinicians can use a number of different strategies to promote parent involvement in the HOPS intervention. Clinicians should attempt to schedule the two HOPS parent meetings at times that are convenient for the parent, such as in the evening or when the parent typically picks the student up from school. For parents who are not able to come to the school, the clinician could offer to complete the parent meetings over the phone. When calling the parent to schedule the first meeting, the parent is more likely to attend if the clinician frames the purpose of the meeting positively. For example, "I have been working with your child on materials organization. I would really like the opportunity to show you all of the great things we are doing. Your child is really making an effort to do better at school and I would like him to share these successes with you." Parents of children with attention and learning problems are typically not accustomed to receiving positive reports from the school. This type of approach is often a welcome change and may make the parent more motivated to attend. It is also important for the clinician to consider how the parent or parents perceive their child's problems. Some parents will not believe that their child has a problem. Alternatively, parents may be feeling completely overwhelmed with their child's issues. The clinician will need to tailor his or her interactions with the parent depending on how the parent presents. Parents who do not believe that their child has a problem may need an extra HOPS session devoted to psychoeducation about the difficulties that children with attention and learning problems commonly experience in the school setting with homework and organization of materials. If a parent seems overwhelmed, the clinician may want to add a session in which the parent is given the opportunity to vent and the clinician just listens. Assessing parents' needs and adjusting the presentation of the material accordingly will help to keep parents engaged throughout the intervention process.

Sometimes parents are not able or are unwilling to be involved with school activities. The HOPS intervention can still be effective in such cases. When parent involvement is low, the clinician can compensate by increasing teacher involvement. In addition, we recommend that the clinician incorporate the HOPS intervention checklists and monitoring procedures into the student's 504 or Individualized Education Program (IEP) following completion of the HOPS intervention. Doing so ensures that school personnel will continue to monitor and reward the student's organization and planning behaviors even after the student is no longer working directly with the HOPS clinician, that is, instead of the parent taking this role.

Teacher Involvement in HOPS

We recommend that clinicians schedule a preintervention meeting with the student's teachers to explain the HOPS program. This initial meeting is important to obtain teacher buy-in for the new organization and homework management systems that the student will be implementing. As part of the HOPS intervention, students will be asking teachers to initial their planners to indicate that homework was recorded accurately. Students will also be implementing a single, 3-inch D-ring binder organization system for managing all class materials. The initial teacher meeting is to provide teachers with an overview of the HOPS intervention and a rationale for the student obtaining the teacher's initials and learning binder organization (see sessions 1 and 2 for further details about the rationale). The supplemental CD-ROM includes an introductory letter that clinicians can send to teachers that briefly describes the HOPS intervention.

Teachers sometimes require that students maintain a specific organization system. For example, a student might be required to maintain a separate binder for science class. In these cases, the clinician should encourage the teacher to allow the student to try the HOPS system for a set period of time (e.g., a 1-month trial). Many times, the teacher's organization requirements can be integrated into the HOPS binder system. For example, the teacher may require that documents such as class notes and worksheets be dated and kept in a particular order. The clinician and teacher might settle on a compromise in which the student dates all papers and keeps them in the teacher's specified order but keeps the class materials within the HOPS binder. It is not critical that the teacher allow students to use the HOPS one-binder system. In the session content, we discuss adaptations that let the clinician complete the organization checklist even if the student is maintaining two or three separate binders.

Teacher update letters are another part of the HOPS manual (see the supplemental CD-ROM) that keeps teachers informed about the skills being taught. These letters are designed to be distributed to teachers at specific sessions when new skills are being introduced to the student. As with parent involvement, the more teachers are involved, the better the intervention outcomes will be. Teachers can provide a unique perspective about how the new organization and homework management systems are working in the classroom. Further, as mentioned above, collaboration with teachers may improve the effectiveness of the reward menu by increasing reward options.

A number of strategies are available that clinicians can use to engage teachers. During the initial teacher meeting, the clinician should try to make the teacher feel part of an intervention team. The intervention should be described as a cooperative effort between the clinician, the student, and the student's parents and teachers. The clinician might engage the teacher by saying, "No one knows better than you about the student's problems with materials organization, so I would really appreciate your input as we work through the intervention." It may be helpful for clinicians to establish a system of communication whereby they briefly check in with teachers about students' progress in the classroom. For example, the clinician could e-mail the teacher a HOPS update every 2 weeks and ask that the teacher reply with how the student is doing in class.

Some teachers will be motivated to learn more about the HOPS interventions. In those cases, the clinician could offer the teacher the opportunity to sit in on a few HOPS sessions. Alternatively, the clinician could offer to share the HOPS treatment manual with the teacher and discuss potential applications to other students in the classroom. Occasionally, a teacher will openly disagree with the idea that a student needs intervention or with the idea that organization and homework management are worthwhile targets for intervention. For example, some teachers will feel that, by middle school, students should no longer need assistance managing their materials. The clinician should use these opportunities to educate the teacher about children with attention problems and about the purpose of the intervention. For example, teachers are often more willing to accept the purpose of the HOPS intervention when it is made clear that the goal is to get students to manage their materials on their own. Specifically, the intervention is short term and uses rewards to rapidly get students to the point that they can manage their own organization and homework responsibilities.

ADAPTATIONS

The adaptations section consists of strategies for implementing the HOPS program in different settings and contexts, for example, as part of a response-to-intervention (RTI) framework (as either a Tier 2 or a Tier 3 intervention). This section also provides information on how clinic-based practitioners and teachers can implement the HOPS program.

HOPS in an RTI Framework

In an RTI framework, decisions about when to intervene and the level of intervention intensity are based on assessment data (Knoff, 2009). To implement HOPS within an RTI framework, the first step is to identify students in the school who are having difficulties with organization and time management. One way to accomplish this is by reviewing teacher grade books and targeting students who have above a certain percentage of missing assignments (e.g., more than 30% of assignments have not been turned in). Alternatively, teachers could simply be asked to identify and refer students who are experiencing organization, planning, and homework management difficulties. There are also measures that do an excellent job of assessing organization and time management skills (e.g., Children's Organizational Skills Scales; Abikoff & Gallagher, 2008b).

An RTI approach also specifies that lower-intensity interventions be tried first with groups of students (i.e., Tier 2), with higher-intensity or specialized interventions (i.e., Tier 3) reserved for those students who do not respond sufficiently (Knoff, 2009). If implemented specifically as suggested in this manual, the HOPS intervention would be considered a Tier 3 intervention. However, the HOPS curriculum can be adapted to serve as a Tier 2 intervention. Intervening with large numbers of students on an individual basis is not feasible from a resource perspective. Accordingly, once a core group of students has been targeted to receive intervention, the HOPS program could first be implemented as a Tier 2 intervention in a small group format, as described below. The clinicians would then set specific mastery or improvement criteria that would indicate students were making sufficient progress with the Tier 2 HOPS program. This is easy to do with the HOPS intervention, as students' progress is documented daily using checklists. Students who did not make improvements on these checklists after a specified period (e.g., 1 month) would be targeted with the Tier 3 HOPS intervention model. Following this RTI-type implementation procedure would allow many more students to receive the HOPS intervention. Two potential adaptations for implementing the HOPS program in small and large group formats are described below.

Small Group Format

The HOPS program could be implemented in its entirety using a small group format with 6 to 8 students per group. Making this work requires two main adaptations. First, the clinician would need an assistant, or a co-leader, to help complete each student's intervention checklists during the session. Second, the time devoted to each session—approximately 20 minutes in the 1:1 model of the HOPS program—would need to be increased to 30 minutes to ensure that there is ample time to complete all of the activities. Further, because students progress through the intervention at different paces, the clinicians would need the extra time to troubleshoot problems individually.

Large Group Format

The HOPS program could also be implemented in a large group format, such as delivered to an entire classroom. As with the small group format, implementing HOPS in large group format would require that at least one other clinician be present. It would also require transferring responsibility for completing checklists from the clinicians to the students. It would take too much time for the clinicians to complete all of the required checklists (organization, teacher initials, and time management) each session for 20–30 students. During the first few sessions, the clinicians would spend time instructing the students on how to complete the checklists. The students would then complete their own checklists during the HOPS group time, under supervision from the clinicians. The students should be told that random accuracy checks will be performed. During these checks, the clinicians would evaluate the accuracy of the students' completed checklists. Students would be reinforced with bonus points for accurate self-completion of the checklists. If accuracy was a consistent problem, the clinicians could implement consequences (e.g., lost points) for inaccurate completion.

HOPS Implementation in a Clinic Setting

Although the HOPS program was designed to be implemented in a school setting, the interventions can easily be adapted for use in a clinic setting. The only component of the HOPS intervention that cannot be implemented in a clinic setting is the locker organization check. However, the clinician can provide the parent with a copy of the organization checklist and arrange for the parent to monitor the child's locker organization. Clinicians will need to work with parents to ensure that the child brings his or her bookbag, binder, and planner to all intervention sessions. If the child arrives at the clinic without these materials, the clinician will not be able to complete much of the session content.

In school settings, the HOPS intervention is designed to be implemented over 16 sessions of 20 minutes each. Given that clinic-based sessions are typically 50 minutes, the intervention would be completed in closer to 12 sessions. We recommend that the intervention not be completed in fewer than 12 sessions, as the pace of skills introduction would likely be too fast for the child. Instead, we recommend that the clinician use the extra time each session to focus on problem-solving, troubleshooting, and transferring the monitoring and reward system to the parent. Typical clinic-based sessions are one time per week, rather than the two times per week suggested in the baseline and training phases of the HOPS program. To account for this, the clinician should instruct the parent to complete the organization and teacher initials checklists at least once per week in addition to the clinician completing the checklists during sessions. This will ensure that the child's progress is monitored and rewarded with the necessary frequency.

In clinic-based settings, the level of parent involvement should be increased from what is recommended in the HOPS manual to counter the fact that the intervention will have significantly less teacher involvement. Further, HOPS rewards should primarily be delivered by the parent rather than the clinician. Thus, during the first few HOPS sessions, the parent, child, and clinician will need to establish a home-based rewards menu to go with the point system. The clinician can also provide rewards (e.g., playing games on the computer for the last 10 minutes of a session) to supplement what the parent is providing. Despite the need for increased parent involvement, we recommend that the clinician meet individually with the child at least four times during the first eight sessions. Meeting individually with the child will help build a strong therapeutic alliance between the child and clinician. Further, parents often have a difficult time remaining constructive when they are present during checklist completion. For example, a parent might get upset that a child has not maintained the organization system and criticize the child during the session. This response can disrupt the session and undermine progress that would have been made through problem-solving. We recommend that the parent start attending every intervention session beginning with the maintenance phase of the HOPS intervention. Having the parent present during all of the maintenance and fading phase sessions will facilitate skills generalization.

Teacher Implementation of the HOPS Intervention

Teachers may not be able to meet with students individually two times per week for 20 minutes each time. Accordingly, teachers will not likely be able to implement the entire HOPS program as it is described in this treatment manual. However, they may be able to focus on one or two of the core skills, such as binder and bookbag organization. In the case of organizational skills training, the teacher would initially need to meet with the child two times for approximately 30 minutes each time to help the child establish the new binder and bookbag system. Once the new system is established, the teacher would need to complete the organization checklist on a regular basis and administer rewards. The checklist and reward meetings would likely last no more than 5 minutes each time. These brief meetings could take place before school, during homeroom or lunch, or immediately after school. We recommend that checklists be completed two times per week until the child meets a predetermined goal (e.g., 80% on the organizational skills checklist). At that time, the teacher can meet with the student to complete checklists once per week.

Chapter 3

HOPS Intervention Session Content

HOPS INTERVENTION SESSION 1 ESTABLISHING A MATERIALS ORGANIZATION BASELINE

SESSION 1 – PRESESSION READING

Session 1 instructs the clinician on how to complete the organizational skills and teacher initials checklists. These checklists will be completed during HOPS session 1 to establish the student's baseline performance on homework recording and materials organization. Session 1 reading also recommends topics the clinician can discuss with the student's teachers before beginning the HOPS intervention.

Introductory HOPS Meeting With the Student's Teachers—Topics for Discussion

As noted in chapter 2, we recommend that the clinician meet with the student's teachers prior to implementing the HOPS intervention. The purpose of this initial meeting is to orient teachers to the intervention and to encourage them to support the student's implementation of the HOPS organization, homework, and planning systems. Clinicians can use the template letter on the supplemental CD-ROM to introduce teachers to the HOPS intervention. Clinic-based providers should mail the introduction letter to the student's teachers. For SMH providers, the initial teacher letter may serve as a guide for a face-to-face meeting. The following are the important points to cover during the initial teacher meeting.

Binder system. As part of the HOPS intervention, students will use one binder for managing all class materials, with sections in the binder for each class or subject. Clinicians should be prepared to explain the rationale behind the HOPS one-binder system. The decision to use a one-binder system is based on clinical experience working with young adolescents with organizational difficulties. Specifically, the more binders, papers, and folders a student tries to maintain separately, the greater the likelihood that materials will get lost or forgotten. With the one-binder system, the student has everything he or she needs for class at all times. Clinicians may also wish to bring an example of a binder to the initial meeting to show teachers. The initial meeting is an opportunity to determine if the one-binder system will work in the teacher's class. Some teachers require students to use class-specific organizational systems, such as a binder specifically for science class. If teachers are hesitant about the student adopting the HOPS binder system, clinicians could suggest a 1-month trial period, with the expectation that if the student's organizational skills do not improve, the student can go back to using the teacher's system. If a teacher is unwilling to allow students to use the HOPS binder system, the clinician should work with the teacher to reach a compromise. For example, the HOPS binder could be adapted to accommodate the teacher's system. The clinician could then agree to add the new criterion to the organizational checklist and to track and reward the student's adherence to the classroom requirement.

Teacher initials and missing assignment tracking. As part of the HOPS intervention, students are required to have teachers initial their planners to verify that the students are recording homework assignments accurately. Teachers are also asked to record in the planner the number of assignments the student failed to turn in that day. If teachers have concerns about these requirements of the HOPS intervention, the clinician can emphasize that the teacher is not being asked to prompt the students (although teachers who would like to prompt a student are welcome to do so). Specifically, in the HOPS program, obtaining teacher initials and information about missing assignments is entirely the student's responsibility. Clinicians may also need to provide a more in-depth explanation of the importance of using teacher initials for children who have problems with organizational skills. A detailed rationale for the teacher initials system is provided in the reading for HOPS session 2.

Information the Clinician Will Be Covering With the Student in HOPS Session 1

During session 1, the clinician will complete a baseline assessment of the student's materials organization system before the intervention. The clinician will use the organizational skills checklist both to complete the baseline assessment and to monitor the student's progress during the intervention. In addition, the clinician will work with the student to establish a rewards menu during session 1 (see the supplemental CD-ROM). Procedures for establishing a rewards menu are described in detail in the "Practical Applications" section in chapter 2. Establishing a rewards menu is necessary if gift cards are not going to be used as the primary reward.

The Organizational Skills Checklist

The example checklist provided on the next page shows what an organizational skills checklist might look like after the session 1 baseline check. The clinician will not spend time fixing the student's organization system or making suggestions during the first intervention session. The clinician is just establishing a baseline.

Completion of the Organizational Skills Checklist

To complete the organizational skills checklist, the clinician will go through the student's bookbag, binder, and locker and record Y or N (yes or no) for each criterion to be met. The clinician should adhere strictly to the checklist criteria definitions. Giving the student positive marks based on the benefit of the doubt at this point will only make it harder for the student to demonstrate progress later. For example, even if there are only two loose papers in the bottom of the bookbag, the clinician should still mark N for that criterion.

In the organizational skills checklist example, the student satisfied some criteria and not others. Under the binder criteria, the student received only one Y (1/7); in the bookbag section, he again met one criterion (1/4); and in the lockers and desks section, he met just one criterion (1/3). Therefore, the student's overall

SUPPLEMENT. Example of a completed baseline assessment using the Organizational Skills Checklist.

ORGANIZATIONAL SKILLS CHECKLIST

	HOPS Session Number
	1
Binder	
Student brought binder to session (if no, student gets binder and mark N for criterion; if student cannot get binder, mark N for all binder criteria).	Y
The student's planner/assignment notebook or the Homework Assignment Tracking Sheet is secured by three rings in the binder.	N
There is a section for each subject the student is taking (e.g., math, science, etc.) and a homework folder in the student's binder.	N
All homework to be completed is in the left side of homework folder and all homework to turn in is in the right side of folder.	N
There are no loose papers in the binder.	N
All papers are in the appropriate class folder/section (e.g., math worksheets are in the math section).	N
No old class papers are in the binder (e.g., no papers from a previous quarter that should be thrown away or filed).	N
Number of binder criteria met (# of Ys/7)	1/7
Bookbag	
If session is late in day: Books needed for homework are in bookbag. If session is early in day: Books needed for class are in bookbag.	Y
There are no books in the bookbag that are not needed for class or to complete homework assignments.	N
There is no loose paper in the bookbag.	N
There are no loose objects in the bookbag (pencils, pens, toys, etc.).	N
Number of bookbag criteria met (# of Ys/4)	1/4
Locker/Desk	
The books are neatly stacked (or shelved) with the spines facing out so that the student can easily grab one in between classes or after school.	N
There are no loose objects (papers, pencils, pens, toys, magazines, etc.).	Y
There is no unnecessary clothing.	N
Number of locker/desk criteria met (# of Ys/3)	1/3

Note. Enter the HOPS session number at the top of the column and then go down the checklist and evaluate the student on each criterion. Record Y (for yes) if the student meets the criterion fully or N (for no) if the student does not meet the criterion fully.

Supplemental Materials: Blank copies of the forms and letters are provided on the CD. Permission is given for individual teachers, administrators, or other school personnel to reproduce any form labeled "Supplement."

organizational total for session 1 was 3/14 (i.e., the number of criteria met, out of the total number of criteria checked that session).

HOPS INTERVENTION SESSION 1 – SESSION CONTENT

Activities to Be Completed

1. Establish and build rapport.
2. Give a positive and enthusiastic presentation of HOPS.
3. Assess student's current materials organization system and establish baseline performance.
4. Develop a rewards menu.

Introducing the Intervention

Students are typically hesitant about attending the first HOPS session and may not want to participate in the intervention at all. Accordingly, the main goal for the clinician during session 1 is to get the student excited about the intervention or at least to "buy into" the importance of participating. This is accomplished by establishing rapport with the student and focusing on the positive aspects of the child's academic functioning and their prospects for success in the intervention.

Establishing Rapport

If the clinician does not already have a relationship with the student, then a significant portion of session 1 will be spent establishing rapport, usually by asking the student about interests, favorite things to do, likes and dislikes about school, and family and friends. Asking questions about likes/dislikes and favorite activities will also be useful later when setting up the reward menu. It might help make the child more comfortable if the clinician tells the student a little about his or her own interests. Finding and highlighting common interests, such as a TV show, sports, or bike riding, can significantly speed up the process of building rapport.

Being Positive

Many young adolescents with organization and time management difficulties hear mostly negative things about their efforts at school and about their academic functioning. The clinician will not develop rapport or gain the student's trust by saying that the student is "failing classes and should be trying harder" or "wouldn't need the intervention if you would just complete your homework." These students have already heard it. Instead, the focus should be on the positives about the intervention, as in the following example:

During these meetings we are going to work on getting your school and homework materials organized. This will make it easier for you to do well in school. I think you will find everything I ask you to do to be pretty easy, and I am sure you will make progress quickly. Plus we are going to reward you for the work you put in during these meetings. Why don't we start by making a list of rewards you would like to earn? Here are some rewards I have used with students in the past.

Assessing the Student's Current Organization System

The first step is for the clinician to assess the student's current use of any organizational systems or strategies before introducing new systems. Many students will already be using a specific organization system or will talk about systems they have tried in the past. Students often believe that these systems are effective and do not need to be changed. Rather than dismissing the student's system as ineffective, it is better to acknowledge the work that the student has put into the system, letting the student describe his or her efforts without discounting them. For example, if the student says he or she writes down homework every night and the clinician knows that is not the case, nothing will be gained from challenging the student on that point. Instead, the clinician may respond with "That's great! The homework system that I am going to show you could make it even easier for you to continue being successful with homework recording." The goal is for the clinician to make it sound as if he or she is building on the student's system rather rejecting the student's system and starting over.

The following are potential questions to ask students about their current materials organization system:

- *Other students I have worked with get tons of school papers and worksheets each week. How do you manage all of those materials? Do you have a system for keeping things straight?*
- *How about homework? Do you write your assignments down, or are you able to remember everything on your own?*
- *How do you know what materials to bring home each day?*
- *Where do you write down your homework?*
- *How are your mom and dad involved in making sure you complete your homework? Do they check your planner after school or check to see that you have the materials you need?*

Performing a Baseline Assessment of the Organization System

Establishing a baseline of students' organization system is important for being able to show the student later how much progress he or she has made. As discussed in the reading for session 1, the clinician should not spend time suggesting ways to fix the student's organization system. The clinician might tell the student, "I am just trying to get an idea of how you currently organize school materials." The clinician can even complete the checklist while talking to the student and building rapport, drawing minimal attention to the checklist completion. For example, "Can I take a look in your bookbag and take some notes while we talk?" If the student asks about the checklist, the clinician can tell the student that he or she will learn how it works at HOPS session 2.

Developing a Rewards Menu

At this point in the session, the clinician should work with the student to begin developing a rewards menu (see chapter 2, the Practical Adaptations section, for information on establishing a rewards menu). The rewards menu does not need to be finished this session, and the clinician and student can update and modify it in future sessions. A template of a rewards menu is provided on the supplemental CD-ROM.

HOPS INTERVENTION SESSION 2
INTRODUCING THE HOPS MATERIALS ORGANIZATION SYSTEM

SESSION 2 – PRESESSION READING

In session 2, the clinician will begin teaching the student the HOPS materials organization system. The purpose of this reading is to provide clinicians with a rationale for the HOPS organization system so that they are prepared to explain the system to the student.

Flexibility of the HOPS Binder System

As described in chapter 2, we recommend that students use a specific binder organization system, including the use of a 3-inch D-ring binder for managing all class materials. The size of the binder is a recommendation, not a requirement of the program. We have found that a majority of middle school–age students can fit all of their core class materials into one 3-inch D-ring binder. In some cases, students may need a 4-inch binder to accommodate all of their materials, and some students have successfully maintained two 2-inch binders. Discussions with the student and the student's teachers can determine what size binder to start with. Some trial and error may be required before it can be determined what binder system will work best.

As discussed in the session 1 reading, some teachers require that students maintain a separate binder and/or notebook for their class. If this occurs, the clinician should talk to the teacher, explain the rationale for the one binder system, and encourage the teacher to allow a trial and error period with the HOPS system. If the teacher is not open to this idea, the clinician will need to check multiple binders at each HOPS session. This is accomplished either by completing two columns on the checklist each time (one for each binder) or by maintaining two separate organizational skills checklists.

Order of Materials in the HOPS Binder

The HOPS intervention specifies the order of materials in the binder. Having a specific and clearly defined structure for the binder allows the clinician to consistently monitor and reward students' progress. In session 2, the clinician should assist the student with establishing the new binder system.

Materials in the binder should appear in the following order:

1. Pencil and pen pouch
2. Planner (or agenda or assignment book), or homework assignment tracking sheets
3. Homework folder labeled "Homework to be completed" on the left and "Homework to be turned in" on the right
4. Dividers with tabs to identify the class name (one for each class)
5. Folders labeled with class name (one for each class)
6. Loose-leaf paper

Use of an Agenda or Planner Versus the Homework Assignment Tracking Sheets

Some schools provide students with class or daily planners. We provide the homework assignment tracking sheet on the supplemental CD-ROM because sometimes the school-provided planners are not designed so students can record homework assignments and obtain teachers' initials. For example, the space where assignments can be recorded is often small, which makes student's writing hard to read. The clinician and student should make a joint decision about which to use. Regardless of the choice, securing the planner or tracking sheet within the three-ring binder will reduce the likelihood that it will get lost.

The Homework Folder

The homework folder goes in the front of the student's binder after the pencil/pen pouch and the planner and is a place for students to keep all homework assignments that need to be completed and turned in. The folder should be secured in the binder (some folders will need to be punched to fit).

Homework to be completed goes in the left side of the folder. Homework to be turned in goes in the right side of the folder. Old homework papers are to be filed in the appropriate class section. Clinicians will monitor and reward students' use of the homework folder using the binder section of the organizational skills checklist.

Implementation of the HOPS Organization System

Working with the student to establish the organization system for binder, bookbag, and locker is straightforward and primarily involves cleaning out all loose papers and materials and either (a) throwing them away, (b) putting them in the three-ring binder, or (c) sending them home with the student (e.g., extra jacket in locker). Two to four 20-minute sessions are devoted to establishing the HOPS organization system. An additional three sessions are devoted to solving any problems the student has with using the organizational system. Depending on how organized the student is before beginning the HOPS intervention, establishing the new binder, bookbag, and locker systems may take only two sessions. The following are some recommended tasks to complete during the organizational sessions.

Session 2. This session will focus on cleaning out old papers from the student's binder and bookbag and introducing the organizational skills checklist. We recommend that these tasks be accomplished before transferring materials to the new binder. In our experience, if the clinician tries to accomplish both tasks in the same session (i.e., cleaning out and transferring to the new binder) the session will go over 20 minutes. When cleaning out the student's old papers it can be difficult to determine what papers need to be kept and filed and what papers can be thrown out. Clinicians are encouraged to use a three-pile system: (a) papers that clearly need to be thrown out, (b) papers of uncertain value, and (c) papers that clearly need to be kept and filed in the appropriate class section. The clinician can then put all papers from pile 2 in a folder and have the student go through the folder with a teacher.

Session 3. For students who are particularly disorganized, much of this session will again be devoted to cleaning out and filing papers. The goal of this session is to finish transferring all of the papers the student needs to keep into the new HOPS binder. If there is time remaining in session 3, the clinician can go to the student's locker or desk to help clean out papers.

Session 4. This session should be devoted to finishing any organizational activities not completed during sessions 2 and 3. If cleanout activities were completed already, session 4 can be spent discussing strategies for maintaining the organization system.

Once the clinician and student have established the student's new materials organization system (binder, bookbag, and locker), the student should meet all of the criteria listed on the organizational skills checklist.

Key Features of the Organizational Skills Checklist System—Monitoring and Rewards

Below is an overview of how the student's organization system will be monitored and rewarded:

- The organizational skills checklist will be completed by the clinician at every session, for that session day (2 times per week initially).
- Students earn 1 point for every "yes" and can earn 11 or 14 organization points each session, depending on whether or not the locker/desk is checked. The clinician should check the student's locker/desk approximately every other session.
- The number of points the student earns will be recorded on the points system tracking sheet (see the supplemental CD-ROM). A detailed explanation of how to complete the points system tracking sheet can be found in the session 3 reading.

HOPS INTERVENTION SESSION 2 – SESSION CONTENT

Activities to Be Completed

1. Complete a second baseline assessment of the student's materials organization system using the organizational skills checklist.
2. Introduce the HOPS binder and bookbag organization systems and the organizational skills checklist. Teach the student how his or her organization will be monitored.
3. Begin working with the student to clean out the student's old system (throwing away and filing papers).
4. If the old system is cleaned up and there is additional time, provide the student with the new binder materials and establish the new materials organization system.

Establishing the Materials Organization System

The clinician should begin the session by completing the second baseline check of the student's materials organization using the organizational skills checklist. The clinician should record the session date and then move down the column checking all criteria. This second baseline check is important to ensure that the first baseline check was not an anomaly. The locker should be checked at least one time, either in session 1 or 2 (lockers tend to have less day-to-day variability in organization).

Introducing the Organization System

Once the second baseline has been established, the clinician should introduce the HOPS materials organization system. As in session 1, the clinician should present the system in a positive way that will increase the likelihood that the student will accept the new way of organizing materials, as in the following script.

It looks like you have a pretty good organization system and have already tried a number of ways of managing your school materials. As part of the HOPS program, we are going to ask that you try organizing your materials a specific way. We have found that this way works really well for most students. The new system may take some getting used to at first, but I think eventually you will find that it is easy to use. We are going to organize your binder, bookbag, and locker so that you meet all of the criteria on this organizational skills checklist perfectly. I have all new school binders, folders, and other materials for you to set up your new system. This is all yours to keep. Once we get your new system set up, we will talk about the rewards you can earn for keeping everything organized.

Introducing the Monitoring and Rewards Procedures for the Organizational Skills Checklist

The following script is an example for introducing how the HOPS materials organization system will be monitored. An example organizational skills checklist, which is provided on the next page, has been completed four times and can be used to illustrate while reading the script.

Once we have finished organizing your binder, bookbag, and locker, you will automatically meet all of the criteria on this checklist. Each time we meet, I will complete this checklist to help keep track of your organization and, more important, to keep track of how many points you have earned toward rewards. The more criteria you meet on this checklist, the more points you will earn.

Here is an example of an organizational skills checklist completed for another student. Where you see the Ys means that I checked the student's organization and he or she met the criteria listed on the checklist. The Ns mean that the criteria were not met. For example, let's look under the binder section. For session 1, which was held on 10/5 [point out the date so that the student can follow along], *the student only received 1 out of 7 possible Ys that day. What did this student receive the one Y for?* [Answer: The student brought his binder to the meeting with the clinician.] *That's right. The student brought his binder to our meeting. It is important that you bring your school binder every time that we meet. You will get 1 point just for bringing your binder when we meet!*

Okay, now let's look at the bookbag section for session date 10/16. This student received three Ys. The student had all the books he needed to complete the next day's homework, which means if this student had a math assignment, then the math book was in the backpack. What was the next thing in the bookbag section that this student had a Y in? [Answer: There are no books in the bookbag that are not needed to complete the homework or for class.] *That's right. This means that magazines and books from subjects in which you have no homework are not in your backpack. This student's final Y was given because he did not have any unnecessary clothing in his backpack—no sweatshirt or t-shirt from last week, no extra pair of socks.*

I am going to reward you for staying organized and using the system I just described. I will check your organization every time we meet. For every Y you receive on your organization checklist, you will get a point, which means you can earn up to 28 points just for organization each week. You will get points for other things as well. We will go over the points system in much more detail next time. I just wanted to give you an idea of how you will get rewards for staying organized.

At this point, the clinician should help the student with cleaning out the binder and bookbag. For students who are particularly disorganized, this may take all of sessions 2 and 3. For students who are already somewhat organized, it may take only one session. As noted in the reading for session 2, we recommend that the old system be cleaned out before materials are transferred to the new binder system. When cleaning out the student's current system, the clinician should query the student about whether or not he or she needs each of the papers and worksheets currently in the binder and bookbag. Any paper that is no longer needed should be thrown out. Any paper that the student needs to keep should be placed in the class folder of the binder or three-hole-punched and placed in the class-specific section of the binder. It is often helpful to have a large recycling bin close by for all of the excess papers thrown out during this process.

SUPPLEMENT. Example of a completed Organizational Skills Checklist.

ORGANIZATIONAL SKILLS CHECKLIST

	HOPS Session Number								
Binder	1 10/5	2 10/9	3 10/12	4 10/16					
Student brought binder to session (if no, student gets binder and mark N for criterion; if student cannot get binder, mark N for all binder criteria).	Y	Y	Y	Y					
The student's planner/assignment notebook or the Homework Assignment Tracking Sheet is secured by three rings in the binder.	N	Y	Y	Y					
There is a section for each subject the student is taking (e.g., math, science, etc.) and a homework folder in the student's binder.	N	N	N	N					
All homework to be completed is in the left side of homework folder and all homework to turn in is in the right side of folder.	N	N	Y	Y					
There are no loose papers in the binder.	N	N	N	N					
All papers are in the appropriate class folder/section (e.g., math worksheets are in the math section).	N	N	Y	Y					
No old class papers are in the binder (e.g., no papers from a previous quarter that should be thrown away or filed).	N	N	N	N					
Number of binder criteria met (# of Ys/7)	1/7	2/7	4/7	4/7					
Bookbag									
If session is late in day: Books needed for homework are in bookbag. If session is early in day: Books needed for class are in bookbag.	Y	Y	Y	Y					
There are no books in the bookbag that are not needed for class or to complete homework assignments.	N	N	Y	Y					
There is no loose paper in the bookbag.	N	N	N	Y					
There are no loose objects in the bookbag (pencils, pens, toys, etc.).	N	Y	N	N					
Number of bookbag criteria met (# of Ys/4)	1/4	2/4	2/4	3/4					
Locker/Desk									
The books are neatly stacked (or shelved) with the spines facing out so that the student can easily grab one in between classes or after school.	N	N	N	Y					
There are no loose objects (papers, pencils, pens, toys, magazines, etc.).	Y	N	Y	Y					
There is no unnecessary clothing.	N	N	N	N					
Number of locker/desk criteria met (# of Ys/3)	1/3	0/3	1/3	2/3					

Note. Enter the HOPS session number at the top of the column and then go down the checklist and evaluate the student on each criterion. Record Y (for yes) if the student meets the criterion fully or N (for no) if the student does not meet the criterion fully.

 Supplemental Materials: Blank copies of the forms and letters are provided on the CD. Permission is given for individual teachers, administrators, or other school personnel to reproduce any form labeled "Supplement."

Transferring Materials to the New HOPS Binder

If the student and clinician clean out the old system and there is time remaining in the session, materials can be transferred to the new HOPS binder. The following gives the order that materials should be placed in the new HOPS binder.

1. Pencil and pen pouch
2. Planner (or agenda or assignment book), or homework assignment tracking sheets
3. Homework folder labeled "Homework to be completed" on the left and "Homework to be turned in" on the right
4. Dividers with tabs to identify the class name (one for each class)
5. Folders labeled with class name (one for each class)
6. Loose-leaf paper

HOPS INTERVENTION SESSION 3 INTRODUCING THE HOPS HOMEWORK MANAGEMENT SYSTEM

HOPS INTERVENTION SESSION 3 – PRESESSION READING

More content is covered during HOPS session 3 than in any other HOPS session. It may be difficult to complete session 3 in 20 minutes, and the clinician may want to allot an additional 15 minutes for this session, if possible. During session 3 the clinician will do the following:

1. Continue to establish the student's materials organization system.
2. Introduce the teacher initials requirement.
3. Introduce the HOPS rewards system and points system tracking sheet.

The majority of session 3 will be spent continuing to establish the new organization system. Introducing the student to the teacher initials requirement and points system tracking sheet will take approximately 10 minutes. It is important that students participating in HOPS be able to earn points and rewards quickly. This is especially important early in the intervention process to help motivate the student to adopt the new skills. Waiting to introduce the teacher initials requirement until a later session would significantly reduce the number of points the student could earn early in the intervention process. For this reason, the teacher initials requirement is introduced in session 3 even though the organization system may not be fully established yet. The session 3 reading is long because we provide a detailed description of the teacher initials and points systems. However, introducing these concepts to students is straightforward and basically involves telling them that they will be asked to get teacher initials in their planner, indicating that they recorded the homework assignment accurately. The clinician should let the student know that he or she will earn 1 point for each teacher initial they receive.

A rationale for the teacher initials system and details of the clinician's responsibilities are provided on the next page. A separate, simplified explanation for the student is provided in the session 3 content.

Rationale for Teacher Initials Homework Management System

Establishing a system for homework management becomes critical during the middle school years and goes hand in hand with the binder system. With multiple teachers assigning homework, it becomes essential that students accurately record homework assignments and record them with sufficient detail. Students are sometimes able to get by without writing assignments down in elementary school by relying on memory. Students quickly learn that "I just remember what is due" is no longer a sufficient strategy in middle school. Further, during this period, young adolescents often start increasing their efforts to deceive their parents regarding homework assignments. Students quickly learn that when mom or dad asks, "Do you have any homework?" if they say no, it means that they get to go outside and play. Parents often don't find out that assignments are being missed and tests inadequately prepared for until it is too late. Some parents go to great lengths to figure out what homework is actually being assigned each night. Parents gather information about assignments and tests in the following ways:

- E-mail teacher
- Call teacher
- Use teacher-provided weekly outline of curriculum that lists all assignments
- Go to website that lists homework assignments and upcoming tests
- Call a phone system through which the teacher updates homework assignments daily

Each of these alternatives requires a significant amount of parent and teacher effort or is not 100% reliable. For example, even when phone or website systems are in place, they may be updated inconsistently by some teachers. Further, teachers are often forced to deviate from curriculum and assignment outlines (e.g., for a snow day or assembly), and the homework information becomes inaccurate. Finally, it requires a significant amount of time and effort for parents and teachers to find common times to communicate with each other daily about homework assignments. This can be overwhelming for a teacher with 20–30 students if multiple families use this strategy. For these reasons, HOPS uses a system of teacher initials to ensure that what the student is recording in their planner is accurate.

For the same reasons outlined above, it can also be difficult for parents to find out if their child failed to turn in homework assignments. It is important for parents to receive this information on a daily basis to prevent missing assignments from piling up and getting to the point where it is too late to turn assignments in (the child would no longer receive credit). Accordingly, in the HOPS program, students are told to ask their teachers to record the number of assignments they missed that day in class in the planner. Teachers can simply write a number (0, 1, 2) next to the initials that they are providing to ensure that homework was recorded accurately.

Use and Monitoring of the Teacher Initials Checklist in HOPS Sessions

The clinician will record whether or not the student received teacher initials on the teacher initials checklist. At every HOPS session, the clinician should record the teacher initials that the student received and the number of teacher initials that were expected (number of core classes) for *all* school days since the last session. For example, if the clinician meets with a student every Monday and Thursday, during the Monday session, the clinician would check the assignment book for the previous Thursday and Friday, and during the Thursday session the clinician would check for the previous Monday, Tuesday, and Wednesday. Students receive 1 point for every teacher initial received. If no homework was assigned in a particular class, the student must write the words "no homework" and have the teacher initial in order to receive credit. A student with four core classes each school day has the opportunity to earn 20 points per week from teacher initials (i.e., 4 points per school day for 5 days = 20 points).

Homework Assignment Tracking Sheet

Fairly often, the clinician will find that the student's school-provided planner is either lost or is not user friendly. For example, sometimes the space provided to record homework assignments for each class is not large enough to record homework, tests, and study methods, as required in later sessions of the intervention. Further, a small space makes it more likely that the student's writing will be illegible. If this is the case, or if the student has lost the agenda, the clinician should provide the student with the homework assignment tracking sheet (see the supplemental CD-ROM). The clinician will need to type in the class names to match the student's core classes. The student should be given at least a 4-week supply of these sheets, which should be three-hole-punched and placed as the first page of the student's school binder (i.e., in place of the planner). The clinician may want to offer these sheets to all students, as some will prefer them even if the school-provided planner is user friendly. One benefit of the homework assignment tracking sheets is that they have a place for recording teacher initials and missing assignments, which serves as a reminder.

Phases of Teacher Initial System

The teacher initials system is in two phases, based on the principal of "freedom through responsibility." Specifically, if a student has demonstrated responsibility for obtaining teacher initials for a set period of time, he or she earns the freedom of no longer needing to get initials. If a student averages a 75% or higher combined percentage for receiving initials averaged over a 2-week period, he or she graduates to phase 2 and is no longer required to obtain teacher initials. Once a student enters phase 2, the clinician should check randomly with the student's teachers (at least once per week) to ensure that the student is continuing to accurately record homework assignments. For example, the clinician could photocopy a page of the student's assignment notebook and show it to the teacher to document accuracy. Another option is for the clinician to check with the teacher before the intervention session to determine what should be written in the student's planner. The clinician should inform any student in phase 2 that if there is a discrepancy between what is recorded and what the teacher says was assigned, then the student will go back to phase 1 until 75% is again achieved for a 2-week period. In phase 2, the student earns the same number of points for recording homework assignments. For example, if the student has four core classes on Monday and recorded homework for all classes, then 4 points would be earned. If no homework was assigned in a class, the student must still write "no homework."

Introduction to the Points System Tracking Sheet

The points system tracking sheet is designed to help the clinician keep track of the points a student earns using the organizational skills checklist, teacher initials checklist, and time management checklist (introduced in session 7). An example of the points system tracking sheet can be seen in the next section.

The points system tracking sheet is organized by HOPS session date. In the teacher initials row, the clinician should record the total number of points for teacher initials that the student has earned since the last session. For example, if the clinician checked the planner for 3 school days, and the student received four initials each day, 12 points (4 × 3) would be recorded in the initials row. In the organization row, the clinician should record the number of points the student earned for that session's completion of the organizational skills checklist. For example, if the student met all criteria on the organizational skills checklist, the clinician would record 14 points. A zero should be recorded in the time management row until the student starts earning time management points (the student would be able to begin earning points for time management starting in session 8). The sum of the materials organization points and teacher initials points should be written in the space for total points earned today. The sum of the points earned today and the points earned from all previous sessions should be written in the space for total points in the bank. When a student cashes in points for a reward, the number of points cashed in should be subtracted from the total points banked.

Example of How to Complete the Points System Tracking Sheet

The example of the points system tracking sheet on the next page, demonstrates how a clinician has used the teacher initials checklist and organizational skills checklist to assign the student points.

During the Monday, October 19, session, the clinician checked teacher initials for the previous Friday, Thursday, and Wednesday, and the student earned a total of 10 teacher initials points (i.e., he received 10 initials during the previous 3 days). The clinician recorded 10 in the teacher initials row under the 10/19 column. During that same session, the clinician completed the organizational skills checklist, and the student earned a total of 11 points (binder, bookbag, and locker points). The clinician recorded 11 in the organization points row. The 10 teacher initial points were added to the 11 organization points, and the sum (21) was recorded in the space for total points earned today. The clinician then added the points earned during the October 19 session (21) to the total points the student had in the bank from the previous session (10/16; 43 points) and recorded the sum (64) in the total points in bank row for the October 19 session.

Assignment of Points

The number of points students can earn for organization and teacher initials is flexible. Clinicians are encouraged to provide additional bonus points to motivate students when needed or when students accomplish goals. This is especially important early in the intervention process. On average, students who are performing well in the intervention will earn around 25 points per week from organizational checks and 20 points per week from teacher initials. This means that a student will earn 100 points in about 2 weeks. Letting students know how many points they can earn, and that they will earn points much faster once time management skills are introduced, will be helpful to them. We recommend that the clinician offer bonus points for 100% completion of teacher initials (four expected and four received) early in the intervention to help motivate the student. For example, in the session 3 content, we recommend that students earn 25 bonus points the first time they receive all of their teacher initials for a particular school day (e.g., four out of four).

Note that teachers also will be recording the number of missing assignments students have each day, in addition to initialing that students have recorded the homework assignment accurately. In the HOPS intervention program, providing rewards for turning in homework (i.e., not missing assignments) is the parents' role. The clinician will introduce this idea to the parent at the first parent meeting that takes place between sessions 5 and 6. Students may ask why teachers are recording missing assignments but they aren't receiving points. Students should be told to that they will start earning rewards for improving missing assignments after the first parent meeting.

HOPS INTERVENTION SESSION 3 – SESSION CONTENT

Activities to Be Completed

1. Continue establishing the HOPS materials organization system.
2. Introduce the concept of the teacher initials system.
3. Introduce the rewards and points systems and the points system tracking sheet.

SUPPLEMENT. Example of a completed Points System Tracking Sheet.

POINTS SYSTEM TRACKING SHEET

	HOPS Session Date					
	10/5	10/9	10/12	10/16	**10/19**	
Earned Today *Teacher Initials*	0	0	13	7	**10**	
Earned Today *Organization*	3	4	7	9	**11**	
Earned Today *Time Management*	0	0	0	0	**0**	
Total Points *Earned Today*	3	4	20	16	**21**	
Total Points *Overall in Bank*	3	7	27	43	**64**	
	HOPS Session Date					
Earned Today *Teacher Initials*						
Earned Today *Organization*						
Earned Today *Time Management*						
Total Points *Earned Today*						
Total Points *Overall in Bank*						
	HOPS Session Date					
Earned Today *Teacher Initials*						
Earned Today *Organization*						
Earned Today *Time Management*						
Total Points *Earned Today*						
Total Points *Overall in Bank*						

 Supplemental Materials: Blank copies of the forms and letters are provided on the CD. Permission is given for individual teachers, administrators, or other school personnel to reproduce any form labeled "Supplement."

Evaluating Materials Organization

The clinician and student may finish establishing the HOPS organization system by the end of session 3. Once the student's organization system is in place, the clinician should use the organizational skills checklist to evaluate the student's new organization system. The student should meet all of the criteria and earn 14 points. The clinician can use the opportunity to introduce the points system tracking sheet by recording the 14 earned points on the points system tracking sheet. Assigning the student 14 points for working with the clinician to develop the new system may help to get the student excited about the new organization system.

Introducing the Teacher Initials System to the Student

Below is an example script to use as a guide for introducing the teacher initials requirement. The clinician should feel free to add details and to modify the script as needed.

Another way you can stay organized is by accurately recording your homework assignments every day in your assignment notebook. I know that you get a lot of homework from multiple teachers, and my job is to help you manage all of this work and get it completed.

For the next few weeks I need you to have all of your main teachers—math, science, history, and language arts—put their initials in your assignment notebook next to the homework assignments you record. That way we can be sure that what you recorded is completely accurate. You have four main, core class teachers, right?

At the end of each class period I want you to record your homework assignments and then go have your teacher initial next to what you recorded. If you don't have any homework that day, you need to write "no homework" and have your teacher initial it. Your teachers can initial really fast as you are walking out of class. I already talked to your teachers about this and they know you are going to be asking. If you get these teacher initials consistently, you will only have to get initials for a couple of weeks. Teachers will also be recording how many missing assignments you had that day, if any (assignments that you were supposed to turn in that day but didn't). We will work with your parents to set up a reward system for the missing assignments.

One benefit of the teacher initials system is that your mom and dad will know that everything you recorded is accurate and they won't have to bug you about it anymore. The main benefit for you is the points. You will be earning points for initials, which will combine with the points you will earn for materials organization. You can trade in these points for rewards from the menu we developed the first time we met.

You will earn 1 point for every teacher initial that you receive. I will be checking your assignment book for all school days, meaning that you can earn an additional 20 points per week for getting teacher initials. This means you will start earning rewards really fast! What do you think?

To help you get started, why don't we say you can earn 20 extra bonus points if you get all of your core class teachers to initial one day this week? If you get them all to initial for two days in a row that would be 40 bonus points, three days in a row would be 60 bonus points! How does that sound?

Additional Details

It is important to tell the student that if no homework is assigned in a class, he or she is required to write the words "no homework" in the assignment notebook and have the teacher initial. No points will be provided for blank spaces, even if the student insists that the teacher did not assign homework in that class.

It is also important that the student and the teachers participating in the initials system know that recording homework assignments is entirely the responsibility of the student. Students are not to ask their teachers to record homework assignments for them. The teacher's only responsibility is to initial the planner after the student has recorded assignments and to write the number of assignments that were missing that day. Further, the teacher does not need to prompt the student. It is important that these points be made clear when the clinician initially presents the system to the student's teachers; otherwise, the teachers may be unwilling to participate.

The clinician should be aware that students will sometimes try to forge their teachers' initials. The clinician should check in with teachers occasionally even when the student is in phase 1 (approximately once every other week) to make sure the initials are not being forged.

An example of a homework assignment tracking sheet that has been completed for one school week, and the corresponding teacher initials checklist, are provided on the following three pages for the clinician to demonstrate how the tracking system works.

Explaining the Points System Tracking Sheet

At this point in the session, the clinician can briefly explain to the student how points will be tracked on the points system tracking sheet. The following script can be used as a guide.

Since you will be earning lots of points, we need a good way to keep track of them. We are going to use this points system tracking sheet to keep track of all the points you earn from organization checks and teacher initials so we know when you earn rewards.

Do you see how the student on this example tracking sheet is earning more and more points each session? This is what you are going to do as you get more familiar with the system. You can see that by session 5, this student had earned 67 total points, and that the student will reach 100 points and earn a reward soon. Before you know it, you will have earned enough points for your first reward! Does this sheet make sense to you? Do you have any questions?

HOPS INTERVENTION SESSION 4
USING THE HOPS SYSTEMS EFFECTIVELY

SESSION 4 – PRESESSION READING

The primary goal of session 4 is to complete any tasks that were described in sessions 2 and 3 of the manual but not completed (e.g., finish establishing organization system or introducing the teacher initials requirement). Once the student's organizational system is fully established and the teacher initials requirement has been introduced, the focus of HOPS sessions should shift to improving proficiency with the systems and solving difficulties. Sessions 4 through 6 are devoted entirely to teaching students strategies for maintaining their organization systems and for improving consistency with homework recording and teacher initials checklists.

SUPPLEMENT. Example of a student's entries on a Homework Assignment Tracking Sheet.

HOMEWORK ASSIGNMENT TRACKING SHEET

Week of _10/15_

Class/Subject	Monday 10/15	Tuesday 10/16	Wednesday 10/17	Thursday 10/18	Friday 10/19
Math	pg. 206 #1-8 Teacher Initials _LR_ # Missing Assign. _NA_	no homework Teacher Initials ___ # Missing Assign. _NA_	pg. 215 #6-12 Teacher Initials _LR_ # Missing Assign. _NA_	no homework Teacher Initials _LR_ # Missing Assign. _NA_	no homework Teacher Initials _LR_ # Missing Assign. _NA_
Science	no homework Teacher Initials _AS_ # Missing Assign. _NA_	Periodic Table quiz! Teacher Initials _AS_ # Missing Assign. _NA_	no homework Teacher Initials _AS_ # Missing Assign. _NA_	Read Ch. 7 Teacher Initials _AS_ # Missing Assign. _NA_	 Teacher Initials ___ # Missing Assign. _NA_
Language Arts	Pick out book from library Teacher Initials _KK_ # Missing Assign. _NA_	Start reading book for report Teacher Initials ___ # Missing Assign. _NA_	no homework Teacher Initials _KK_ # Missing Assign. _NA_	no homework Teacher Initials _KK_ # Missing Assign. _NA_	Poetry Day! Teacher Initials _KK_ # Missing Assign. _NA_
Social Studies	Executive Branch worksheet Teacher Initials _KS_ # Missing Assign. _NA_	no homework Teacher Initials _KS_ # Missing Assign. _NA_	Study Ch. 8 Teacher Initials _KS_ # Missing Assign. _NA_	worksheet Teacher Initials _KS_ # Missing Assign. _NA_	TEST! Teacher Initials _KS_ # Missing Assign. _NA_

Note. The teacher's initials indicate that the homework assignment was recorded accurately; # missing assignments = the number of assignments not turned in that should have been.

 Supplemental Materials: Blank copies of the forms and letters are provided on the CD. Permission is given for individual teachers, administrators, or other school personnel to reproduce any form labeled "Supplement."

SUPPLEMENT. Example of a completed Teacher Initials Checklist.

TEACHER INITIALS CHECKLIST

Date	10/15	10/16	10/17	10/18	10/19			
Initials Received	4	2	4	4	3			
Initials Expected	4	4	4	4	4			
Points Earned	4	2	4	4	3			
Date								
Initials Received								
Initials Expected								
Points Earned								
Date								
Initials Received								
Initials Expected								
Points Earned								

Note. Teacher initials are tracked for ALL school days, not just for HOPS session days. Accordingly, the dates filled in by the clinician should be the dates of all school days, not HOPS session dates. Initials Received – The clinician should record the number of teacher signatures in the student's planner on that particular school day. Initials Expected – This is the number of initials the student should have received that day (typically, the number of core classes). Points Earned – In the HOPS program, students earn 1 point for each teacher initial received. However, the clinician has flexibility in assigning points and can provide bonus points for meeting interim goals. If a student averages 75% (e.g., 3 received out of 4 expected or better) for a 2-week period, circle the date, and the student may stop asking for teacher initials.

Supplemental Materials: Blank copies of the forms and letters are provided on the CD. Permission is given for individual teachers, administrators, or other school personnel to reproduce any form labeled "Supplement."

SUPPLEMENT. **Example of a completed Points System Tracking Sheet.**

POINTS SYSTEM TRACKING SHEET

	HOPS Session Date					
	10/5	10/9	10/12	10/16	**10/19**	
Earned Today *Teacher Initials*	0	0	13	7	**13**	
Earned Today *Organization*	3	4	7	9	**11**	
Earned Today *Time Management*	0	0	0	0	**0**	
Total Points *Earned Today*	3	4	20	16	**24**	
Total Points *Overall in Bank*	3	7	27	43	**67**	
	HOPS Session Date					
Earned Today *Teacher Initials*						
Earned Today *Organization*						
Earned Today *Time Management*						
Total Points *Earned Today*						
Total Points *Overall in Bank*						
	HOPS Session Date					
Earned Today *Teacher Initials*						
Earned Today *Organization*						
Earned Today *Time Management*						
Total Points *Earned Today*						
Total Points *Overall in Bank*						

Supplemental Materials: Blank copies of the forms and letters are provided on the CD. Permission is given for individual teachers, administrators, or other school personnel to reproduce any form labeled "Supplement."

Structure of Sessions 4–6

No new skills are introduced in HOPS sessions 4 through 6. Below is a recommended structure for those HOPS sessions.

- Complete teacher initials checklist and record points (0–5 minutes).
- Complete organizational skills checklist and record points (5–10 minutes).
- Troubleshoot and solve difficulties (10–20 minutes).

The clinician's reading sections for sessions 4–6 are primarily devoted to describing strategies for helping students maintain their organization and homework systems and suggestions for solving commonly occurring difficulties with system implementation. The session 4 reading section presents two strategies for promoting consistency with teacher initials: visual prompts and a specific initials plan. The clinician will probably not have enough time to create the visual reminders and to establish a specific plan for obtaining initials during session 4. The clinician should prioritize one of these activities and plan on completing the other activity in session 5.

The first parent meeting should occur between sessions 5 and 6. A significant portion of session 5 is devoted to preparing for the first parent meeting. The meeting should last approximately 1 hour and should be attended by the student and the parent or parents. The purpose of the meeting is to orient the parent to the HOPS program and to have the parent establish a system for rewarding improvements in missing assignments. The clinician may want to schedule the parent meeting at this point.

Consistency in Obtaining Teacher Initials

Initially, most students will have a difficult time remembering to ask teachers to initial their planners. When class ends, students are focused on gathering materials and getting to their next class quickly. Many students will simply forget to ask teachers for initials. For that reason, we encourage clinicians to work with students to establish a visual reminder system. The key is to put visual reminders where the student is likely to see them frequently. Below we provide a few recommendations for possible visual reminder systems.

The clinician should consider writing the words "Get Teacher Initials!" in bold lettering on the top of every page in the student's planner or homework assignment tracking sheets. Alternatively, the clinician can have the student write and decorate a similar prompt. For example, the student could use a marker or colored pen and draw a small picture next to each reminder statement. Having the student write and decorate the prompt might promote the student to take more responsibility for the process. However, a reminder prompt in the planner will work only if the student consistently opens the agenda each class period.

If the student does not routinely use the planner, the clinician will need to consider alternate locations for the visual prompts. For example, if the student consistently uses the three-ring binder in each class, a visual reminder prompt could be slipped under the front cover of the binder. The student could draw a picture that included the words "Get initials and earn points." Another option is to tape or glue a prompt to the bottom of existing pictures that might already be in the student's binder. For example, students frequently have pictures of their favorite bands or athletes in the front of the binder. If there is not a place to put prompts on the outside cover of the binder, placing a prompt on the cover page of the item that comes first inside the binder also works well.

If the student does not consistently use any materials during class, the clinician will need to place prompts either in the classroom itself or in areas outside of the classroom. Although this solution is not ideal, it is better than having no visual prompts. For example, the student could decorate a picture with a prompt that could be taped to the inside of the locker. If the student sits in the same desk every day in class, the visual prompt could be taped to a corner of the desk.

Establishment of a Specific Plan for Obtaining Teacher Initials

Clinicians should work with students to establish a plan for how and when they will obtain teacher initials. The plan should describe specifically when during the class period the student plans to ask the teacher for initials and how the student plans to ask. In some cases, teacher input will be important in establishing this plan. For example, some teachers have multiple students in the class who ask for initials and have a set time during the class period when planners are reviewed and signed. The clinician and the student may need to develop separate plans for each core class. For example, the student might need to ask for initials at the end of the class period for one teacher and immediately after school before getting on the bus for another teacher. The clinician should encourage the student to establish a plan for getting teachers' initials so the student can feel in control of the process. Recommendations for how to work with the student to develop a plan are provided in the session 4 content.

Progress Graphing

At this point, students should be meeting more criteria on the organizational skills checklist than they were meeting at baseline. Graphing students' progress may help motivate them to continue making improvements. It may also help identify areas in which system adjustments are required. Once graphs are established, they require minimal time and effort to maintain from week to week. The session 13 reading shows detailed information on how to graph students' progress using the HOPS checklists.

HOPS INTERVENTION SESSION 4 – SESSION CONTENT

Activities to Be Completed

1. Finish establishing the materials organization system.
2. Explain the HOPS teacher initials and points systems in greater detail if there was not time for this in session 3.
3. Complete the organizational skills checklist and record points.
4. Complete the teacher initials checklist and record points.
5. Create visual reminders for the student to get teacher initials or establish a specific teacher initials plan.

Reviewing the Student's Progress With the System So Far

The clinician should take some time to review the progress the student has already made in establishing a new materials organization system and to orient the student about what will occur during the next few HOPS sessions. The student has been asked to make lots of significant changes in a short period of time. It may help to reassure the student that no new skills will be introduced because the next few weeks will be spent primarily on improving the organization and teacher initials systems so that the student can earn rewards more quickly.

Establishing a Plan for Obtaining Teacher Initials

The following are open-ended questions the clinician can ask to help the student develop a plan for obtaining teacher initials and to get him or her to think about the process. The clinician should let the student develop the plan and should provide minimal input at this stage. In subsequent sessions, the clinician and student will review how well the plan is working and the clinician will then have the opportunity to suggest revisions to the plan. The clinician should document the initial plan in writing, mainly as a reminder of what the student and clinician decided.

1. *How are you feeling about the teacher initials system?*
2. *Do you think you will be able to get teachers to initial your agenda?*
3. *Tell me about how you will get teachers to initial your agenda? When will you ask them to initial?*
4. *Can you think of anything that might be difficult about getting teacher initials?*
5. *How will you remember to ask teachers to initial?*
6. *How might you ask your teachers to initial? What would you say?*

HOPS INTERVENTION SESSION 5 DEVELOPING A HOME-BASED REWARD SYSTEM

HOPS INTERVENTION SESSION 5 – PRESESSION READING

The primary goal of session 5 is to prepare the student for the parent meeting that will take place between sessions 5 and 6.

Preparation for the First Parent Meeting

The recommended format for the parent meeting is to have one or both parents meet with the clinician and student. The clinician should expect the meeting to last approximately 1 hour. The two main goals for the first parent meeting are to (a) introduce and explain the HOPS intervention; and (b) establish a home-based system for rewarding reductions in the number of assignments the student failed to turn in each school day (i.e., missing assignments). During the parent meeting, the student will be asked to explain the organization and homework systems. Part of session 5 will be used to prepare the student to make this presentation. The student will use the organizational skills, teacher initials, and points system checklists to guide the presentation.

During session 5, the clinician is encouraged to find out from the student how much the parents already know about the HOPS intervention. Having this background information will help the clinician estimate how much time to spend describing the HOPS intervention during the parent meeting. For example, does the parent know that the student is implementing a specific materials organization system? Does the parent know about the rewards system?

The clinician should be prepared to open the parent session by presenting a broad overview of the HOPS intervention. The clinician should cover the basic structure of the HOPS intervention and the core skills targeted. For example, the clinician could tell the parent how many sessions there are, how long each session lasts, and the overall goals of the program. The clinician can then have the student describe the details of the intervention, including the checklists and points systems.

Rationale for a Home-Based Missing Assignment Tracking System

The clinicians' primary role in the HOPS intervention is to teach the student skills necessary for academic success—organizational, homework management, and time management—and how to maintain those skills. To promote students' use of the skills, the clinician provides rewards for skills implementation. At no point in the HOPS intervention does the clinician provide rewards for actual academic improvement.

We purposely did not have the clinician reward improved grades for two reasons. First, in the HOPS intervention, the clinician is already expected to provide rewards for three separate skills and behaviors: materials organization, teacher initials, and time management. Clinicians have a limited range of rewards available to them. It would be very difficult to develop a broad enough rewards menu to make salient reward options available for additional behaviors (e.g., improved test scores). If additional behaviors were added to the rewards system, the student would probably choose one or two skills or behaviors to work on and would not make an effort with the remaining skills.

Second, improvements in academic performance take longer to occur than improvements in skills use. For example, a student can quickly demonstrate and be rewarded for improvements in organizational skills, whereas improvements in test scores or report card grades may take months. As noted in the introduction, long-term rewards are rarely effective. It would be difficult to motivate students to participate in the HOPS intervention if they had to wait for midterm or semester grades to receive rewards. Further, the student's parents have probably offered rewards for improved school grades in the past. Students have likely experienced a repeated pattern of trying and failing to improve school grades. As such, students are often hesitant to make additional efforts if the target is improved grades.

Establishment of a Home-Based Assignment Completion Rewards System

One of the primary goals of the first parent meeting is to establish a system for the parent to reward the student consistently turning in homework assignments. Tracking missing assignments provides the opportunity for the student to earn frequent (daily) rewards for actual improvements in academic performance. Having the parent provide rewards for the student consistently completing and turning in assignments greatly increases the availability and saliency of the reward options (i.e., the parent has access to a range of rewards) and allows the clinician to focus on rewarding skills improvement.

Given the limited amount of time the clinician will have with the parent, it is important that the home-based system be as simple and easy to implement as possible. The system that we recommend is outlined below. For the system described below to work, a parent needs to be willing and able to check the student's planner daily after school. The parent should check the planner as soon as possible after the student arrives home from school. When the parent checks the planner, three potential scenarios could occur: (a) The student did not have all of his or her core class teachers record missing assignments in the planner (i.e., one or more teachers did not review the planner or the student did not bring the planner home). (b) The student had all of the core class teachers record missing assignments in the planner and had one or more missing assignments. (c) The student had all of the core class teachers record missing assignments in the planner and did not have any missing assignments that day.

A reward or consequence should be attached to each of these scenarios. The reward or consequence used will need to be determined in collaboration with the parent. Regardless of the reward chosen, the consequence for scenario 1 should be greater (i.e., more severe) than the consequences for scenarios 2 and 3. The following are alternative rewards or consequences for the three scenarios.

Alternative 1. Student did not have all core class teachers record missing assignments in the planner (i.e., one or more teachers did not review the planner or the student did not bring the planner home). Reward or consequence—Student must complete 1 hour of homework before being allowed to engage in any other activities (e.g., no TV, video games, or free time outside before 1 hour of work is completed).

Alternative 2. The student had all core class teachers record missing assignments in the planner and had one or more missing assignments. Reward or consequence—Student must complete a half hour of homework before being allowed to engage in any other activities. If possible, the time should be spent completing the missing assignments.

Alternative 3. The student had all core class teachers record missing assignments in the planner and did not have any missing assignments that day. Reward or consequence—Student is allowed 1 or 2 hours of free time before needing to come in and complete homework.

There are two important considerations for making this system work. First, the amount of free time the student is allowed for option 3 must be the same or ideally more than what he or she is currently receiving each day after school. Second, for options 1 and 2, the parent must be prepared to assign work if the student says that there is none to be completed. One option is for the student to outline a chapter in a textbook. The chapter the parent chooses should be based on what the class is currently working on and what information will be covered on the next test. Another option is for the student to complete worksheets with relevant current class material. The clinician can often help the parent get access to these types of worksheets by asking teachers.

The parent should leave the meeting with the home-based plan for tracking missing assignments in writing. The missing assignments tracking plan template on the supplemental CD-ROM will guide the development of the plan. The clinician can print the template out and complete it during the parent session. The parent will likely have questions when implementing the rewards system at home. The clinician may want to schedule a phone call for 1 week after the parent meeting to make sure that the parent is implementing the system correctly and to answer questions.

HOPS INTERVENTION SESSION 5 – SESSION CONTENT

Activities to Be Completed

1. Complete the organizational skills checklist and record points.
2. Complete the teacher initials checklist and record points.
3. Create visual reminder prompts for getting teacher initials or develop the specific teacher initials plan.
4. Prepare for the parent meeting.

Preparing the Student for the Parent Meeting

If the clinician and student did not have time to create visual reminder prompts and to develop the teacher initials plan in session 4, these tasks should be prioritized during this session. Once those tasks are accomplished, the clinician can introduce the student's part in the parent meeting using the following script.

The next time we meet will be for our first parent meeting. I want to ask you some questions to get an idea of how much your parents know about what we have been working on. Have you talked to your [mom/dad] about what we have been working on? What have you told them or shown them? Have your parents been helping you to stay organized or reminded you to get teacher initials? Did you tell your [mom/dad] anything about the rewards you will be earning?

I would like you to take the lead during the parent meeting. I would like you to show your [mom/dad] the organization, teacher initials, and points system checklists we have been using and explain to them how they work. How about if we go through each of the checklists now as practice? Can you briefly explain each of them to me? [Go through each checklist with the student, having them explain each to you.] Great job, your [mom/dad] is going to be so impressed with how much you have learned.

HOPS INTERVENTION PARENT MEETING 1

HOPS INTERVENTION PARENT MEETING 1 – SESSION CONTENT

The clinician should strive to keep the tone of the parent meeting positive and focused on the student's efforts and progress to date. For many students, interactions with parents related to organization and homework are mostly negative. Students grow accustomed to this negative pattern of interaction and come to dread talking about these issues with their parents. The clinician can begin to break this cycle by starting with an introduction that will set a positive tone for the meeting.

Example Introduction and Overview

Below is an example of how the clinician could introduce the purpose of the HOPS parent meeting.

Thank you for coming. [Student's name] has been working very hard to improve organization and homework management. First, I want to give you with a brief overview of the HOPS intervention program. Then I would like to have [student's name] tell you about the homework and organization system [he or she] has started implementing. Then we will spend the rest of the meeting talking about ways you might be able to support [student's name] new homework management skills at home.

At this point the clinician should provide a brief overview of the structure and purpose of the HOPS intervention. The clinician can then prompt the student to share the organization, teacher initials, and points system checklists. Some students will be able to do the presentation on his or her own, whereas others will need the clinician to interject and to clarify or prompt the student to provide more detail. Below are examples of ways the clinician can support the student's presentation.

Student – *Ms. X [the clinician] checks my homework and I get points if I record it right.*

Clinician – *That's right. Can you tell your mom how often we check homework and how I know that you recorded your assignments accurately?*

Student – *My planner is checked two times a week, and I get teacher initials showing that I recorded my homework accurately.*

Clinician – *Can you tell your mom about the teacher initials checklist and what these numbers mean?*

Student – *This sheet says how many initials I got out of how many I needed to get. I need to get initials for all of my main classes.*

Some parents will try to interject with negative statements such as: *"Why didn't you get all of your teacher initials on this day?"* The clinician should redirect the parent whenever possible by making statements such as: *"It always takes a while for students to get used to the system and for us to figure out the right rewards. Typically, students improve gradually over time."*

Once the student and the clinician have explained the homework, organization, and points systems, the parent should be given the opportunity to ask questions. Sometimes parents will express concerns related to providing students with rewards. Parents may make statements such as: *"In my day it was just expected that you complete your homework. You didn't get anything extra for being responsible."*

These types of statements are an opportunity for the clinician to teach the parent about the purpose of reward systems. For example, the clinician might say something like the following:

"It sounds as if you want [student's name] to be internally motivated to complete these tasks, and that is our goal too. However, we find that students have to experience success first before internal motivation takes over. Often, students start to feel as if, no matter what they do with their homework management, it is never good enough for their parents or teachers. After a while, they stop trying or put in minimal effort. The same thing sometimes happens to adults at work. For example, what would happen if no matter what effort you put in, your boss said it was not good enough? We are trying to set clear and realistic goals and to show [student's name] that [he or she] can achieve them. We are providing some extra motivation in the form of rewards to get [him or her] started down the right path. The internal motivation you are talking about will take over when [student's name] sees that being organized and managing homework well has resulted in better grades and parents who are proud."

Introduction to the Missing Assignments Tracking Plan

In the remainder of the session, the clinician should focus on developing a home-based rewards system for the student for completing assignments. Using the script below as an example, the clinician should try to get the parent to commit to a specific home-based system, and the system should be recorded in as much detail as possible on the missing assignments tracking plan sheet. At the end of the session, the clinician should provide the parent with a copy of the plan (see the missing assignments tracking plan template on the supplemental CD-ROM).

As we discussed, I will be providing rewards for [student's name's] progress with organization and homework management. As a result of working on these skills, [student's name] may start to decrease [his/her] number of missing assignments. We are hoping that you will be willing to help [student's name] improve academic performance by providing rewards at home for decreasing the number of missing assignments. [Student's name's] teachers are (or will be) recording the number of assignments missed each day in the planner. It would be great if you could review the planner after school to see how [he/she] is doing with missing assignments. Do you think that would be possible?

Great! When [student's name] shows you [his/her] planner, there are really three options for how it could look. These options are listed on this sheet [show parent the missing assignments tracking plan]. Let's review three different things that could happen each day after school when you check the planner.

"It would be great if you could provide a reward or consequence for each of these options. One idea I had was that [student's name's] schedule after school would depend on which of these criteria he/she met. Basically, depending

on which criteria were met, he/she would either have to complete homework first before any other activity or could have free time first."

At this point, the clinician should work with the parent to formalize a rewards or consequences plan and to complete the missing assignments tracking plan sheet. The reward options discussed in the session 5 reading can be used as a reference.

HOPS INTERVENTION SESSION 6
MAINTAINING THE ORGANIZATION SYSTEM

HOPS INTERVENTION SESSION 6 – PRESESSION READING

The primary goal of session 6 is to review and discuss the parent meeting with the student and to continue solving any problems with the organization and teacher initials systems. If enough time has passed, the clinician should inquire about the implementation of the home-based system. For example, has the parent been checking the planner and, if so, has the parent consistently been providing rewards or consequences. The remainder of the session should be spent identifying and solving any problems. Session 6 is the last session devoted entirely to these skills, because time management skills are introduced in session 7. Below are some strategies for helping students to maintain their materials organization system.

Maintenance of the Materials Organization System: Establishing a Specific Plan

Students rarely have established routines for organizing their own materials. Prior to experiencing the HOPS intervention, the student's materials probably got more and more disorganized each week until a parent or teacher noticed and forced the student to clean out his or her bookbag or binder. This may have occurred once per month or once per semester. To be successful with the organization component of the HOPS intervention, the student will need to develop a routine for maintaining his or her system of organizing materials. If the student were to use HOPS intervention sessions to maintain the system (i.e., the student and clinician would clean out the student's binder and bookbag each session), the materials would stay organized, but the student would never learn to maintain the materials organization system on his or her own. During session 6, the clinician should work with the student to develop a plan for maintaining the materials organization system.

Key Components of the Materials Organization Plan

To remain organized, the student will probably need to file and throw away papers at least once per week outside of intervention sessions. The plan should include the following key components and should be recorded in detail on the materials organization plan sheet provided on the supplemental CD-ROM:

- When (date and time) will the student complete the self-organization checks and clean-up process?
- Where will the self-organization checks occur?
- What exactly will happen during the check? What will be checked and how?
- How will the student remember to complete the checks?

The student should take the lead on generating ideas for maintaining the organization system so that he or she takes control of the process. The session 6 content section includes an example script for developing an organization plan and a template for documenting the key components of the organization plan.

Evaluation of the Effectiveness of the Rewards System

It is important for the clinician to continually evaluate the effectiveness of the points system and rewards menu. If the student is not obtaining initials consistently or is not maintaining the organization system, one of two things is likely occurring: either the rewards are not meaningful enough to the student, or the student is not earning rewards frequently enough. If the clinician determines that the rewards are not salient enough and the student doesn't really care about earning the rewards, the clinician should work with the student to revise the options on the rewards menu. If the student is not earning rewards frequently enough, then the points earned for each skill should be increased, or the point values needed to earn rewards should be decreased. For example, to encourage the student to obtain teacher initials, the clinician might revise the points system so that the student earns 5 points for each initial and needs to earn 50 points for a reward instead of 100. In some cases, the clinician will need to pursue both options—that is, revising and adding to the rewards menu and changing point values—to effectively motivate the student.

HOPS INTERVENTION SESSION 6 – SESSION CONTENT

Activities to Be Completed

1. Complete the organizational skills checklist and record points.
2. Complete the teacher initials checklist and record points.
3. Review the parent meeting.
4. Develop a specific plan for maintaining the materials organization system.

Encouraging the Student to Develop an Organization Plan

Below is an example conversation between a student and a clinician. In this example the clinician is encouraging the student to establish a specific plan for maintaining materials organization.

"I hate to see you miss out on points by having loose papers in your binder each time we meet. What could you do to make it more likely that you won't have loose papers next time?" The student will likely respond in general terms: *"I could clean it first."* To which the clinician might respond: *"That is a great idea. When might you do that?"* The clinician should then take out a blank copy of the materials organization plan sheet (see the supplemental CD-ROM) and show the form to the student. *"Let's use this form to record your ideas about staying organized during the week."* The clinician then continues to ask the student questions until the materials organization plan sheet is completed. For example, *"How would you remember to clean it?"* If the student's response is too general, the clinician may need to prompt for a more specific response. For example, the clinician might say *"Maybe we could make a visual reminder for you that you would be sure to see. What is something that you look at every day at home? Maybe something in your room, such as your bedroom door or the TV? How about if we make a sign to tape on [whatever object the student chooses] that says 'Clean out binder and bookbag on [specific day chosen]?' Does that sound like a good plan? Let's use this materials organization plan sheet to write down some more of your ideas."*

After completing the materials organization plan sheet, the clinician is encouraged to establish a bonus reward for the student's coming to sessions and meeting all of the binder or bookbag criteria on the organizational skills checklists. This can be a one-time reward to help the student get motivated to clean out the binder and/or bookbag in between HOPS sessions. For example, the clinician might offer the student 25 bonus organization points for the first time he or she comes to a HOPS session with no loose papers and all papers filed in the correct section of the binder.

HOPS INTERVENTION SESSION 7
PLANNING AND STUDYING FOR TESTS

HOPS INTERVENTION SESSION 7 – PRESESSION READING

The primary goal of session 7 is for the clinician to introduce time management and planning skills. The clinician will teach the student how to use a planner to prepare effectively for upcoming tests and quizzes. Students will be able to earn extra points for accurately recording dates of future tests, what the tests will cover, and how they will study for the tests.

Mastery of Organization and Teacher Initials Versus Introduction of New Skills

Moving on to time management skills does not imply that all students will have mastered binder, bookbag, and locker organization and teacher initials at this point in the HOPS intervention. In fact, a majority of students will not have mastered these skills and activities. At this point in the intervention, we expect a good deal of variability in students' performance on the organizational skills and teacher initials checklists from session to session.

Even if it seems that minimal progress has been made with organization and homework recording, there are three reasons why the clinician should begin teaching time management skills. First, materials organization and homework recording skills are not prerequisites for effective use of time management skills. For example, a student can use the agenda to plan for tests and quizzes even if he or she is not receiving teacher initials consistently. As such, students can benefit from using time management skills even if they are not consistently using the organization and initials systems. Second, adding time management skills creates an opportunity for the student to earn more points and to earn points more quickly. This may help motivate some students to improve performance across all aspects of the HOPS intervention. Third, teaching time management skills does not mean the clinician will no longer be able to help the student improve organizational skills and homework management. The clinician will continue to closely monitor these skills by completing the two checklists at all intervention sessions.

Introduction to Time Management Skills

We recommend that the clinician use a two-step process for introducing time management skills. First, the clinician should introduce the skill by going over each of the relevant criteria on the time management checklist and explaining how points are earned for each criterion. Second, the clinician should practice the skill with the student. Whenever possible, the clinician and student should use actual assigned schoolwork (i.e., an upcoming test or project) to practice the skill. The student must demonstrate an understanding of how to implement each skill and how points are earned. This in-session practice will prevent potential misunderstandings and disagreements about what is required to earn points. It also gives the clinician confidence that the student truly understands how to use the skills. We recommend that the clinician motivate the student by assigning points the first time a student practices a skill in session. In the session 7 content section, we provide an example script for having the student practice the test and quiz planning skills.

Completion of the Time Management Checklist Test and Quiz Sections

The time management checklist is divided into four sections: (a) test and quiz recording, (b) test and quiz studying, (c) long-term projects, and (d) evening schedule. The test and quiz portion of the checklist is separated into two distinct sections: test and quiz recording and test and quiz studying. The criteria from the test and quiz portion of the time management checklist are listed below. After each criterion is an example of a behavior that would meet that criterion and earn the student points. The projects and evening schedule portions of the checklist are covered in subsequent sessions.

Test and Quiz Recording
1. Student recorded an upcoming test or quiz in the planner at least 1 day in advance in general terms. The student earns 2 points each time he or she records that a test is scheduled for a particular day in the planner. For example, the student might write the words "spelling test" in the planner on the day that the test is scheduled to occur.

2. Student recorded an upcoming test or quiz in the planner at least 1 day in advance in specific terms. The student earns 3 points for not only recording that a test is scheduled but also recording what the test will cover. Using the example provided above, the student would need to write "spelling test on vocabulary list 20" to meet this criterion.

Test and Quiz Studying
1. Student designated a time to study for an upcoming test at least 1 day in advance of the test. This can be recorded without specific details about what will be studied (e.g., "study for spelling test"). The student must at a minimum record the word "study" at least one day in advance of the test. The student earns 4 points.

2. Student designated a time to study and recorded the amount of time to study. The student who meets this criterion is essentially assigning homework. For example, if the student has a test on Friday and on the Wednesday before recorded "study spelling words for 15 minutes," the student would meet this criterion and would earn 5 points.

3. Student designated a time to study and recorded the study method. For example, the student would meet the criterion if he or she recorded anything like the following: make flash cards, review flash cards, make outline of chapter 6, write definitions, or have mom or dad quiz me. The student would earn 6 points.

4. Student designated a time to study and recorded the amount of time and method. This criterion is a combination of criteria 4 and 5 and earns the student 7 points.

Guidelines for Completing the Time Management Checklist

Students earn points for the highest criterion met in each section. For example, in the test and quiz recording section, if a student records an upcoming test and records specifics about what the test will cover, the student would earn 3 points, not 2 points plus 3 points.

Students can meet the same criterion (e.g., recording specific details about a test) for multiple class subjects in the same day. If a student writes "test today" for science and "test" for math, the student has recorded an upcoming test in general terms for two separate classes and should earn 4 points (2 points for each class). Because students can earn points for multiple class subjects, the clinician should record the subject name or abbreviation in the space next to the criterion (e.g., Sci. or LA) rather than a checkmark. This will allow the clinician to document that a student met a particular criterion for two separate classes.

Checking of the Student's Planner for Time Management Criteria

On the next two pages is an example of a completed time management checklist (test and quiz recording and studying sections) and an example of a student's planner. The planner provides examples of what a student might record related to upcoming tests and quizzes and what time management criteria would be met. The clinician should initial the student's planner when the student has been given points to avoid confusion in subsequent sessions about what has already been reviewed.

In this example, at a session on Monday 11/1, the clinician checked the student's planner for the entire week (i.e., looking ahead). The student met criterion 2 in test and quiz recording and criterion 2 in test and quiz studying and earned a total of 8 points.

HOPS INTERVENTION SESSION 7 – SESSION CONTENT

Activities to Be Completed

1. Complete the organizational skills checklist and record points.
2. Complete the teacher initials checklist and record points.
3. Introduce the time management checklist test and quiz sections.
4. Practice test and quiz recording and planning.
5. Solve any problems.

Introducing the Concept of Planning for Tests

After completing the checklists, the clinician can introduce the time management checklist to the student using the following script.

You have been doing really well with getting teacher initials and keeping your materials organized. I want to challenge you a little bit and give you the opportunity to earn more points. So far you have mostly been recording homework assignments in your planner. Now I want to see if you can record upcoming tests and quizzes too. We are also going to see if you can use your planner to prepare for studying for quizzes and tests. You will have the opportunity to earn a lot more points every time you record information about how and when you are going to study for tests. How does that sound?

Introducing the Time Management Checklist

The next script shows examples of how to meet each criterion.

There are six ways that you can earn points for recording information about tests and quizzes in your planner. Each of the ways you can earn points is listed on this time management checklist [show student the example].

SUPPLEMENT. Example of a student's entries on a Homework Assignment Tracking Sheet.

HOMEWORK ASSIGNMENT TRACKING SHEET

Week of _11/1_

Class/Subject	Monday _11/1_	Tuesday _11/2_	Wednesday _11/3_	Thursday _11/4_	Friday _11/5_
Math	Study Math for 1 Hour Teacher Initials ___ # Missing Assign. ___	Teacher Initials ___ # Missing Assign. ___	Math Test Today on Chapters 5 & 6 Teacher Initials ___ # Missing Assign. ___	Teacher Initials ___ # Missing Assign. ___	Teacher Initials ___ # Missing Assign. ___
	Teacher Initials ___ # Missing Assign. ___	Teacher Initials ___ # Missing Assign. ___	Teacher Initials ___ # Missing Assign. ___	Teacher Initials ___ # Missing Assign. ___	Teacher Initials ___ # Missing Assign. ___
	Teacher Initials ___ # Missing Assign. ___	Teacher Initials ___ # Missing Assign. ___	Teacher Initials ___ # Missing Assign. ___	Teacher Initials ___ # Missing Assign. ___	Teacher Initials ___ # Missing Assign. ___
	Teacher Initials ___ # Missing Assign. ___	Teacher Initials ___ # Missing Assign. ___	Teacher Initials ___ # Missing Assign. ___	Teacher Initials ___ # Missing Assign. ___	Teacher Initials ___ # Missing Assign. ___

Note. The teacher's initials indicate that the homework assignment was recorded accurately; # missing assignments = the number of assignments not turned in that should have been.

Supplemental Materials: Blank copies of the forms and letters are provided on the CD. Permission is given for individual teachers, administrators, or other school personnel to reproduce any form labeled "Supplement."

SUPPLEMENT. **Example of a completed Time Management Checklist.**

TIME MANAGEMENT CHECKLIST

		HOPS Session Date							
		11/1							
Test & Quiz Recording	**Points**								
1. Student recorded an upcoming test or quiz in planner at least 1 day in advance in *general terms* (e.g., test today).	2								
2. Student recorded upcoming test or quiz in planner at least 1 day in advance in *specific terms* (e.g., listed pages covered).	3	Math							
Test & Quiz Studying	**Points**								
1. Student *designated a time to study* for an upcoming test at least 1 day in advance of the test (e.g., study for test today).	4								
2. Student designated a time to study and recorded the *amount of time* to study (e.g., study for science, 30 minutes).	5	Math							
3. Student designated a time to study and recorded the study *method* (e.g., outline chapter 4 or make flash cards for math).	6								
4. Student designated a time to study and recorded the amount of time *and* method (e.g., study flash cards for 20 minutes).	7								
Long-Term Projects	**Points**								
1. Student recorded in planner an upcoming project at least 1 week in advance of project due date.	4								
2. Student recorded in general terms a specific day to work on a project at least 1 day in advance of due date (e.g., work on project).	5								
3. Student recorded a specific day to work on a project at least 1 day in advance of due date and listed a specific activity (e.g., research topic on computer).	6								
4. Student broke down a project into at least two separate tasks and assigned deadlines for each (e.g., do computer research by 6/12/10 and write rough draft by 6/22/10).	7								
Evening Schedule	**Points**								
1. Student completed an evening schedule.	3								
2. Student recorded a specific amount of study time or homework time on the evening schedule.	4								
3. Student recorded a specific amount of study or homework time and recorded the specific activities to be completed.	5								
Total Time Management Points Earned		8							

Note. Students earn points for the highest criterion met in each section of the checklist. Record the class subject for which the criterion was met in the blank: Math, Science, History, or Language Arts. Students can earn points for the same criterion for multiple class subjects (e.g., records an upcoming test in specific terms for both science and math = 6 points earned, 3 points for each class).

 Supplemental Materials: Blank copies of the forms and letters are provided on the CD. Permission is given for individual teachers, administrators, or other school personnel to reproduce any form labeled "Supplement."

First, let's look at criterion 1 in the recording section which says, "Student recorded an upcoming test or quiz in planner at least one day in advance." Let's say that on Monday your teacher tells you that on Wednesday you will have a math test. If you go into your planner and in the Wednesday math space write "Math test today," you would meet criterion 1 and earn 2 points.

If instead of just writing "Math test today," you recorded what the test covered ("Math test today on chapter 6"), you would meet criterion 2 in that section and earn 3 points. If you did that for both science and math class, you would earn 6 points.

The next section has to do with how you are planning to study for tests and quizzes. To meet criterion 1 in the studying section, you would need to write in your planner that you were going to study for the math test. For example, if your math test was on Wednesday and in the Tuesday math space in your planner you wrote "study for math test," you would earn 4 points. Writing that you are going to study really shows me that you are planning for the test.

If you record the amount of time that you are going to study for the upcoming test or quiz, you earn 5 points. For example, let's say that on Monday, you put in your assignment book that you have a math test on Wednesday and that it is on chapter 6. You also record the words "study 30 minutes for math test" in the math slot on Tuesday. You would earn 3 points for recording when your test is and what it will cover and another 5 points for recording that you will study and how much time you will study.

The next criterion is similar except that instead of writing how much you are going to study, you would record how you are going to study. Can you give me an example of a method someone might use for studying? [Possible answers are read over notes, read over the chapters the test covers, make flashcards]. *Very good! What is the method you usually use to study for tests? Sticking with our math test example, if you wrote "make flash cards for math test" or "outline chapter 6 for math test," you would earn 6 points.*

To meet the last criterion in that section, you need to write both how much time you are going to study and the method of studying you are going to use. You would earn 7 points for doing both.

The nice thing about these time management skills is that you can earn points really fast. If you met the highest criterion in the studying section for all four of your classes (math, language arts, history, and science), you would earn 28 points in one day! Think of how fast you will earn rewards between your organization, teacher initials, and time management checklists. Do you have any questions?

Practicing for Test and Quiz Recording and Planning

At this point in the session, the clinician should practice test and quiz recording with the student. An example script is provided below to guide this discussion.

Let's go ahead and practice test and quiz recording and planning now. We can work through the process of planning for one of your upcoming tests together. We can even go ahead and assign you points for practicing the skill. How does that sound?

When is the next time that you will have a test or a quiz in any of your classes? If the student does not know of any upcoming tests or quizzes, the clinician should make up an example. However, most students have weekly or biweekly spelling tests, and the clinician can prompt to see if this is the case. *Great, so you have a test on [day] in [subject]. Is that test recorded in your agenda? If not, why don't you go ahead and write it in. Do you know exactly what the test will cover, the pages or chapter? If so, you can write in the specifics of what the test will cover. Either way is fine. If you write in the specifics, you earn 3 points; if not, you still earn 2 points. Now let's work together to plan for the test by recording when you will study in your planner. Then we will work through the process of assigning you points.*

The clinician's goal should be to have the student do as much of the planning and writing as possible. The clinician can accomplish this by asking open-ended questions and only providing suggestions when necessary.

Okay, so you have a test on [day]. How much time would you normally study for a [subject] test? It is important that you be honest with me so that we can set a realistic goal for studying for this next test. Okay, so you would normally study [X] minutes for a test like this. Is that how much you would like to study this time? Okay, so you want to study [X] minutes for this test, when would you like to do that? Okay, so go ahead and record in your planner that you would like to study on [X] day and record how many minutes you plan to study. Great. You already earned 5 points for doing that, plus the [2 or 3] you earned for recording the test. If you wanted to earn more than 5 points, what would you need to do? You can look at the time management checklist if you want. That's right. If you recorded the method you are going to use to study (basically, how you are going to study), you would earn more points. How do you usually study for tests? Does that work well for you? Okay, let's record the method you are going to use for this test in your agenda. Great. Now you have earned 7 points! Let's go ahead and add those points to your points system tracking sheet. Do you have any questions about what we just did? Great. If you record that type of information in your agenda from now on, you will earn time management points every time we meet.

HOPS INTERVENTION SESSION 8
PREPARING TO COMPLETE LONG-TERM PROJECTS

HOPS INTERVENTION SESSION 8 – PRESESSION READING

The primary goal of session 8 is to introduce the long-term projects section of the time management checklist. As with the test and quiz section, we recommend that the clinician have the student practice long-term project planning in session using an actual school project. The clinician will also complete the test and quiz sections of the checklist and assign points during session 8.

The long-term projects section of the time management checklist is similar to the tests and quizzes section and is designed to encourage students to plan ahead for the completion of long-term projects. The projects section and tests and quizzes section are distinct, and a student can earn points in both sections in the same HOPS session. As with the test and quiz sections, the criteria definitions build, with the more complex skills earning the student more points. Students earn points for the highest criterion that they meet in each section. Students can meet the same criterion multiple times in a single HOPS session. For example, if a student recorded when a long-term project was due in social studies and also one for science, he or she would earn 4 points for both and a total of 8 long-term project points.

Completion of the Time Management Checklist (Long-Term Projects Section)

The section below describes the criteria in the long-term projects section of the time management checklist and gives examples.

1. Student recorded in planner an upcoming project at least 1 week in advance of project due date. The student does not need to write specifics to meet this criterion. The student can simply write "science project." The student should record this information on the date that the project is due. The student earns 4 points.

2. Student recorded in general terms a specific day to work on a project at least 1 day in advance of the due date. The student can record this information in general terms, for example, "work on science project," as long as the information is recorded in the agenda at least 1 day before the project is due. For example, let's say the clinician and the student have a HOPS session on March 16. The clinician notes that the student recorded the words "science project" in the planner for April 5 (the day the project is due). The clinician then notes that in the student's planner on the April 1 date, the student wrote "work on science project." The student meets this criterion and earns 5 points.

3. Student recorded a specific day to work on a project at least 1 day in advance of due date and listed a specific activity. This is the same in all aspects as the previous criterion except that the tasks to be completed are listed in specific rather than in general terms. In the example provided above, if the student wrote "research the topic on computer" or "complete rough draft of paper," the student would meet this criterion and earn 6 points.

4. Student broke down a project into at least two separate tasks and assigned deadlines for each. This is the same as the previous criterion except that the student needs to separately record at least two specific tasks. The tasks must be listed on separate days. For example, if the student wrote "complete computer research" on April 1, and "develop an outline for the paper" on April 3, the student would meet the criterion and earn 7 points.

Example of Completed Time Management Checklist (Long-Term Projects Section)

On the next page is an example of a student's planner, and the corresponding example of a completed time management checklist (long-term projects section), showing what was written.

Description of Completed Time Management Checklist (Long-Term Projects Section)

In the example, the clinician and student met on October 30, and the clinician checked the student's planner. The clinician looked forward (the next 2 weeks) to see if the student had recorded any information about planning for tests or projects. The clinician observed that the student had written down "book report due!" in the Friday, November 12, slot and also that the student had written "outline key points for book report" in the Wednesday, November 3, slot and "write rough draft for book report" in the Wednesday, November 10, slot. Accordingly, the student reached the highest criterion in the long-term projects section. The clinician recorded "LA" for language arts next to the appropriate criterion under the correct session date. The clinician recorded 7 points in the total points earned space. If the student had also earned points in the test and quiz sections, the clinician would have added those points to the long-term projects points and recorded the total. The clinician would then transfer the total time management points earned to the points system tracking sheet.

The clinician should initial in the planner next to anything (e.g., a test or project recorded) that has been reviewed in a HOPS session. This will ensure that each project recorded in the agenda is reviewed and assigned points only once.

SUPPLEMENT. **Example of a student's 2 weeks of entries on a Homework Assignment Tracking Sheet.**

HOMEWORK ASSIGNMENT TRACKING SHEET

Week of 11/1

Class/Subject	Monday 11/1	Tuesday 11/2	Wednesday 11/3	Thursday 11/4	Friday 11/5
Language Arts			Outline key points for book report		

Week of 11/8

Class/Subject	Monday 11/8	Tuesday 11/9	Wednesday 11/10	Thursday 11/11	Friday 11/12
Language Arts			Write rough draft for book report		Book report due!

Note. The teacher's initials indicate that the homework assignment was recorded accurately; # missing assignments = the number of assignments not turned in that should have been.

 Supplemental Materials: Blank copies of the forms and letters are provided on the CD. Permission is given for individual teachers, administrators, or other school personnel to reproduce any form labeled "Supplement."

SUPPLEMENT. Example of a completed Time Management Checklist.

TIME MANAGEMENT CHECKLIST

		HOPS Session Date							
		10/30							
Test & Quiz Recording	**Points**								
1. Student recorded an upcoming test or quiz in planner at least 1 day in advance in *general terms* (e.g., test today).	2								
2. Student recorded upcoming test or quiz in planner at least 1 day in advance in *specific terms* (e.g., listed pages covered).	3								
Test & Quiz Studying	**Points**								
1. Student *designated a time to study* for an upcoming test at least 1 day in advance of the test (e.g., study for test today).	4								
2. Student designated a time to study and recorded the *amount of time* to study (e.g., study for science, 30 minutes).	5								
3. Student designated a time to study and recorded the study *method* (e.g., outline chapter 4 or make flash cards for math).	6								
4. Student designated a time to study and recorded the amount of time *and* method (e.g., study flash cards for 20 minutes).	7								
Long-Term Projects	**Points**								
1. Student recorded in planner an upcoming project at least 1 week in advance of project due date.	4								
2. Student recorded in general terms a specific day to work on a project at least 1 day in advance of due date (e.g., work on project).	5								
3. Student recorded a specific day to work on a project at least 1 day in advance of due date and listed a specific activity (e.g., research topic on computer).	6								
4. Student broke down a project into at least two separate tasks and assigned deadlines for each (e.g., do computer research by 6/12/10 and write rough draft by 6/22/10).	7	L.A.							
Evening Schedule	**Points**								
1. Student completed an evening schedule.	3								
2. Student recorded a specific amount of study time or homework time on the evening schedule.	4								
3. Student recorded a specific amount of study or homework time and recorded the specific activities to be completed.	5								
Total Time Management Points Earned		7							

Note. Students earn points for the highest criterion met in each section of the checklist. Record the class subject for which the criterion was met in the blank: Math, Science, History, or Language Arts. Students can earn points for the same criterion for multiple class subjects (e.g., records an upcoming test in specific terms for both science and math = 6 points earned, 3 points for each class).

 Supplemental Materials: Blank copies of the forms and letters are provided on the CD. Permission is given for individual teachers, administrators, or other school personnel to reproduce any form labeled "Supplement."

HOPS INTERVENTION SESSION 8 — SESSION CONTENT

Activities to Be Completed

1. Complete the organizational skills checklist and record points.
2. Complete the teacher initials checklist and record points.
3. Complete the tests and quizzes section of the time management checklist and record points.
4. Introduce the long-term projects section of the time management checklist.
5. Identify and solve any problems.

Introducing the Long-Term Projects Section

The clinician should show the student a time management checklist and review each of the long-term projects criteria definitions. The following script can be used as a guide for introducing the long-term projects section.

Last week we learned about ways to plan for tests and quizzes. This week we are going to work on planning for long-term projects. You will be able to earn even more points by recording in your planner when upcoming projects are due and how you plan to work on them.

The projects section of the time management checklist consists of four criteria. Just like the tests and quizzes section, these skills build, and the more information you record, the more points you earn.

Let's look at the first criterion in this section, which says, "Student recorded in planner an upcoming project at least 1 week in advance." Let's say your language arts teacher tells you that a book report is due in 1 month. As soon as your teacher tells you this, you write "LA book report due today" in your planner. You write it on the day the book report is due. You would earn 4 points for that.

The next criterion says, "Student recorded a specific day to work on a long-term project at least 1 day in advance of the due date." To meet this criterion, you would have to record something like "work on book report" in your planner before it was due. You are basically setting aside some time that you plan to work on the book report in advance of when it is due, thinking ahead and giving yourself a homework assignment. This really shows me you are planning, and you would earn 5 points.

The next criterion says, "Student recorded a specific day to work on a project at least 1 day in advance of the due date and listed a specific activity to be completed." This means you are recording exactly what part of the project you plan to complete. For example, if you wrote "finish rough draft of book report" or "complete computer research for book report," you would meet this criterion and earn 6 points.

The last criterion in this section reads, "Student broke down a project into at least two separate tasks and assigned deadlines for each." For example, if you recorded "complete computer research" on one date in your planner and "finish rough draft" on a later date in the planner, you would meet this criterion and earn 7 points.

Remember, you can earn time management points for projects in all four of your main classes. The more information you record, the better. Do these criteria make sense to you? Do you have any questions about them? Every time we meet, I will be checking your planner for any tests and quizzes you recorded and for any projects you recorded. I will add the points you earned for each section together and record the total at the bottom of the page.

Let's go ahead and practice long-term project recording and planning. Do you have any projects or book reports that you have been assigned that we could use for practice?

HOPS INTERVENTION SESSION 9
USING AFTER-SCHOOL TIME EFFICIENTLY

HOPS INTERVENTION SESSION 9 – PRESESSION READING

The primary goal of session 9 is to introduce the evening schedule, the final section on the time management checklist.

Introduction to the Evening Schedule

In session 9, the clinician will work with the student to complete an evening schedule. The student should plan the day after school. The clinician should interview the student to obtain accurate information regarding what time he or she gets home from school, eats dinner, and goes to bed. All of these events should be recorded on the evening schedule. For all other activities (e.g., free time and homework time), the clinician should simply act as a scribe and record the student's projected after-school plan. For example, if the student says that homework that evening will probably take 10 minutes and the clinician suspects that homework will take 1 hour, the clinician should not address the issue at this point. The clinician will help the student develop a more accurate evening schedule during session 10. The clinician should keep a copy of the evening schedule.

Completion of the Time Management Checklist Evening Schedule Section

Below we present the criteria on the evening schedule portion of the time management checklist and briefly describe what a student would need to record to meet each criterion.

1. Student completed an evening schedule. A student earns 3 points if he or she fills out an evening schedule but does not note on the evening schedule when homework or studying will take place.

2. Student recorded a specific amount of study time or homework time on the evening schedule. A student earns 4 points if he or she completes an evening schedule and designates specific periods of time to complete homework or to study for a test.

3. Student recorded a specific amount of study or homework time and recorded the specific activities to be completed. A student earns 5 points if he or she completes an evening schedule that designates time to complete homework or to study *and* describes in the notes section the specific tasks that will be accomplished.

Starting with session 10, students can earn points for bringing completed evening schedules to the HOPS session (see evening schedule template on the supplemental CD-ROM). To receive points, the student must complete the evening schedule ahead of time, demonstrating that the student planned after-school activities in advance. For example, if the clinician and student meet during school on Wednesdays, the student would receive credit for bringing a completed evening schedule outlining his planned after-school activities for that day (Wednesday). He or she could also bring an evening schedule to the Wednesday HOPS session detailing activities to be completed after school on Thursday or Friday. Students will not be able to complete the evening schedule too many days in advance because they won't know what homework will be assigned or how long it will take.

Students receive points for each evening schedule completed. The student may bring multiple completed evening schedules to a HOPS session and should receive points for each one (e.g., if the student completed an evening schedule for Tuesday and Wednesday after school and brought them both to the session on Thursday). If a student brings more than one evening schedule and meets a particular criterion multiple times, the clinician should record ×2 or ×3 in the blank next to the criterion on the time management checklist. The clinician should make a mark on the student's evening schedule (e.g., clinician's initials) so it is clear which evening schedules have already been reviewed.

The example provided on the next page shows a completed evening schedule that meets the highest criterion on the time management checklist and earns the student 5 points.

HOPS INTERVENTION SESSION 9 – SESSION CONTENT

Activities to Be Completed

1. Complete the organizational skills checklist and assign points.
2. Complete the teacher initials checklist and assign points.
3. Complete the tests and quizzes and projects sections of the time management checklist and assign points.
4. Introduce the time management checklist, evening schedule section.
5. Solve any problems.

Introducing the Evening Schedule

The script below can be used to describe the evening schedule section of the time management checklist.

You have worked really hard to keep all of your materials organized and to make sure all of the correct assignments are recorded in your planner each day. One thing we haven't talked much about is what goes on after school when you actually have to complete all of those assignments. Can you tell me a little about how you currently spend your time after school?

What does a typical day look like for you when you get home from school? What activities do you usually complete after school? When do you usually complete homework? For example, do you complete it right when you get home or do you have free time first and finish homework after dinner?

This evening schedule sheet is designed to help you plan out your afternoons on days you know you are going to be particularly busy. As practice, let's use this evening schedule sheet to plan your day after school today.

The clinician should record each of the student's responses on the evening schedule (see the template on the supplemental CD-ROM).

What time will you get home from school today? What will you do first? How long do you think that will take? What will you do after that? How long do you think that will take? What time do you usually eat dinner? How long do you typically spend eating dinner? What will you do after dinner? What time do you usually get ready for bed? What time do you go to bed?

SUPPLEMENT. Example of entries in an Evening Schedule.

EVENING SCHEDULE

Time	Activity	Notes
4:30	Snack	
5:00	Dance class	
5:30	Dance class	
6:00	Dinner	
6:30	Dinner	
7:00	Complete science homework.	Answer questions in the textbook at the end of chapter 6.
7:30	Complete science homework.	Finish answering chapter 6 questions.
8:00	TV	
8:30	TV	
9:00	Study spelling words.	Make flashcards from spelling list on page 76 and review cards for 15 minutes.
9:30	Shower	
10:00	Bed	

 Supplemental Materials: Blank copies of the forms and letters are provided on the CD. Permission is given for individual teachers, administrators, or other school personnel to reproduce any form labeled "Supplement."

The clinician should continue asking questions until the evening schedule is completed.

Introducing Points Earned for Completion of Evening Schedules

The following script can be used to describe how the student can earn points by completing the evening schedule.

Now let's talk about how you can earn points for completing evening schedules like the one we just finished. You might have seen last session that there are three more criteria on the time management checklist that we haven't talked about yet. These criteria are all related to the evening schedule. Look at this checklist.

The first criterion says "Student completed an evening schedule." This means that if you come to any of our sessions with an evening schedule sheet filled out, you will earn 3 points. The purpose of the evening schedule is to show me that you are planning your time after school. To get credit for the schedule, you have to complete the evening schedule ahead of time. For example, you could complete a schedule right now for tomorrow after school if you knew what your homework was going to be.

To meet the second criterion, along with completing the evening schedule, you also need to block out a specific amount of time you will work on homework. As long as you have at least one 30-minute interval devoted to completing homework, you will receive credit and receive 4 points.

For the last criterion, you will need to write in the notes section of the evening schedule the specific homework or studying activities that you plan to complete. This is what you already do in your planner to earn points. For example, you would designate a specific time to study for a test in the left column and then in the right column you would write how you are going to study for the test. For example, you might write "make flash cards" or "read chapter 6."

The clinician should show the student the completed evening schedule found in the presession reading section to illustrate exactly what the student needs to write to meet the criteria. At the end of the session, the clinician should tell the student to pay attention to the activities completed that day after school and how long each activity actually takes. The clinician should tell the student that during the next session they will review the evening schedule that was completed this session to see how accurate it turned out to be.

HOPS INTERVENTION SESSION 10 REFINING THE AFTER-SCHOOL ACTIVITIES PLAN

HOPS INTERVENTION SESSION 10 – PRESESSION READING

The primary goal of session 10 is to identify and solve problems students might have with implementing time management skills and to review the evening schedule that was completed last session.

Review of the HOPS Intervention Time Line

Only two sessions are left (sessions 10 and 11) in the training phase of the HOPS intervention. Session 12 begins the maintenance phase of the HOPS intervention. During the maintenance phase, the clinician will meet with the student one time per week instead of two times per week. In addition, the second and final parent meeting is scheduled to occur between sessions 13 and 14, approximately 3 weeks away. The clinician should consider calling the parent to schedule the second parent meeting at this point.

Review of the Evening Schedule

During session 9, the clinician and student worked together to complete an evening schedule. In session 10, the clinician and student will review the evening schedule completed during session 9 and discuss whether the student was able to adhere to the schedule. The purpose of this conversation is to allow the clinician to help the student become more accurate in planning after-school activities. Below are a few suggestions to engage the student in this discussion.

The clinician should start generally, asking the student open-ended questions such as *"How did it go? Did anything unexpected come up?"* The clinician should then produce the evening schedule completed during session 9 and review each of the activities listed, step by step. The clinician can ask, *"You estimated that you would get home around 3:30 p.m. What time did you get home? You thought that it would take 10 minutes to complete the homework and that you would get it done before dinner. When did you complete that homework and how long did it take?"*

Once the evening schedule has been reviewed, the clinician and student will work together to create a new evening schedule (for that day after school), incorporating changes from what was learned with the first evening schedule.

HOPS INTERVENTION SESSION 10 – SESSION CONTENT

Activities to Be Completed

1. Complete the organizational skills checklist and record points.
2. Complete the teacher initials checklist and record points.
3. Complete the entire time management checklist and record points.
4. Review the evening schedule completed during session 9.
5. Complete a new evening schedule.

Developing the Second Evening Schedule

The first time the clinician worked with the student to complete an evening schedule (session 9), minimal guidance was provided. In this session, the clinician and student will work together to complete another evening schedule. This time the clinician should provide more guidance to shape the student's planned evening schedule. The goal is for the student to (a) learn to more accurately estimate how long after-school activities will take, and (b) begin to modify their after-school schedule to complete schoolwork in the time estimated. Below we provide an example script for guiding students to develop a more accurate and productive evening schedule.

You did a nice job planning your activities after school using the evening schedule. Some things went exactly as you had planned and other things didn't work out the way you thought they would. I would like to work with you to create another evening schedule to plan your after-school activities today. We can use what we learned from creating the first evening schedule to make this one even better.

You said that you ended up completing homework right before bed instead of before dinner as you had planned. What are the benefits of completing homework before dinner? [Suggest that maybe the student gets to watch his or her favorite TV show after dinner.] What are the benefits of completing homework right before bed? Is completing homework before dinner something that you would like to try accomplish today after school? Okay, let's write that on your evening schedule. What could you do to remind yourself to start working on homework before dinner?

You allotted 10 minutes to complete homework on your last evening schedule. From what you said, it sounds as if it took closer to 1 hour. Did you underestimate the time it would take or did something get in the way of you finishing quickly? It can be hard to estimate how long homework might take. Maybe you could block off 1 hour every night and plan for that in your evening schedule. If it takes you less than 1 hour, you can either get in some extra work or you can have extra free time. What do you think? How much time would you like to schedule for homework today after school?

HOPS INTERVENTION SESSION 11 REFINING THE ORGANIZATION AND HOMEWORK PLANS

HOPS INTERVENTION SESSION 11 – PRESESSION READING

The primary goal of session 11 is to revisit the student's materials organization and teacher initials plans and to make adjustments as necessary.

Review of Progress With the Materials Organization and Teacher Initials Plans

In session 4, the clinician and student developed a specific plan for obtaining teacher initials, and in session 6 a plan was developed for maintaining the student's materials organization system. The clinician probably has not had much time to revisit and revise these plans. No new skills are taught in session 11, and this session is a good time for the clinician to check in with the student about the materials organization and teacher initials plans.

Changes do not necessarily have to be made to the plans if the student is performing well with materials organization and teacher initials. Even if no changes are made, revisiting the plans will give the clinician the opportunity to praise the student's progress and reinforce the fact that maintenance of these skills remains important.

Revision of the Teacher Initials Plan

In general, we recommend that changes be made to the teacher initials plan at this point if the student has not yet achieved the goal of greater than 75% completion of teacher initials over a 2-week period. Recall that if students receive more than that level, they are allowed to stop getting teacher initials. The goal of 75% is reasonable because a student with four core classes could miss approximately one teacher initial every day and still achieve the goal. Accordingly, if a student has not achieved the 75% goal at this point in the HOPS intervention, it is likely that the system or plan needs to be adjusted.

If the student's performance with initials is below 75%, the clinician should talk to the student about barriers he or she may face. Many students are dealing with a combination of barriers rather than just one. A few of the common barriers are embarrassment (not wanting to be seen by peers), forgetfulness (has a hard time remembering to get initials), lack of time (can't make it to the next class in time), and lack of motivation (doesn't make an effort).

Below are some potential solutions for overcoming each of these barriers. It is important to keep in mind that the overarching goal of teacher initials is to ensure that the student is recording homework consistently and accurately. In our experience with the HOPS intervention, occasionally students who are not obtaining teacher initials are in fact recording homework accurately and consistently. In these cases, we would recommend that the clinician drop the teacher initials requirement and, instead, reward continued accuracy with homework recording. Specifically, the clinician would check with teachers occasionally (e.g., weekly) to ensure that homework is being recorded accurately. The clinician would then provide 1 point for every homework assignment recorded in the planner instead of 1 point for each teacher initial.

Embarrassment. The student does not like peers observing him or her asking for initials. To solve this barrier, the clinician and student should find a time that the student can ask for initials when peers are not present. It may be important to bring the teacher into this discussion. For example, the student might ask for initials after school. Alternatively, the student might leave the planner with homework recorded open on the desk. The teacher can come by and sign without the student having to ask and without drawing attention to the process. Another option is for the clinician to drop the teacher initials requirement and instead reward the student for accurate and consistent homework recording. A system would be established in which the clinician checks with teachers weekly about homework that should be recorded in the planner. The clinician should check with teachers on a random schedule (e.g., a different day each week) so that the student cannot anticipate when he or she needs to be accurate. The student would then earn points for having the correct assignments recorded in the planner.

Forgets. The student doesn't mind getting initials but has a hard time remembering. To solve this barrier, the clinician and student should revise the prompt or reminder system put in place during session 4. The prompts likely need to be placed in a more visible location. Alternatively, teachers might agree to prompt the student.

No time. The student says that there isn't enough time to obtain teacher initials. The clinician and student could work out a system that allows the student to get the agenda signed before the end of class. The teacher will probably need to be included in this discussion. For example, the teacher might agree to sign the planner during class if the student makes sure that the agenda is complete and open on the front corner of the desk.

Motivation. The student really isn't making an effort to obtain teacher initials and is not recording homework in the agenda accurately or consistently. In this case, dropping the teacher initials requirement is not a viable solution because the student is not recording homework accurately. When motivation is the problem, the clinician will need to either increase the number of points earned for initials or increase the saliency of the reward options offered on the reward menu. For option 1, the clinician could consider offering the student 50 bonus points for achieving above 75% initials over a 1-week period. For option 2, the clinician may need to involve the student's parents. The student's parents have access to a much wider range of reward options. In the second parent meeting content, we provide examples of rewards parents may be willing to offer to supplement the clinician's rewards.

Revision of the Materials Organization Plan

During session 6, the clinician and student established and recorded a specific plan for maintaining the materials organization system. During session 11, the clinician should review this plan with the student. If the student is maintaining the materials organization system from week to week (e.g., consistently misses no more than one criterion on the organizational skills checklist), the plan does not need to be revised. However, if the student is having difficulties maintaining the materials organization system (e.g., has loose papers in the binder and bookbag each week or is not using the homework folder), then the organization plan should be revised. The clinician should go through the organization plan with the student point by point to determine what aspects of the plan are not working.

In our experience with the HOPS intervention, the most common barrier is the student failing to remember to complete the organization clean-up each week outside of HOPS sessions. When this is the case, the clinician should consider adding more highly visible prompts and reminders or increasing the points the student can earn for meeting 100% of the organization criteria in a HOPS session. With respect to prompts and reminders, the clinician will have the opportunity to ask the parents to help with prompts or reminders at the next parent meeting. For additional points, the clinician is encouraged to offer 25 or 50 bonus points the next time the student comes to a HOPS session and meets 100% of the criteria on the organizational skills checklist.

HOPS INTERVENTION SESSION 11 – SESSION CONTENT

Activities to Be Completed

1. Complete the organizational skills checklist and record points.
2. Complete the teacher initials checklist and record points.
3. Complete the time management checklist and record points.
4. Review and revise materials organization and teacher initials plans.

The primary goal of this session is to review and revise the student's teacher initials and materials organization plans that were established in sessions 4 and 6, respectively. The review and revision process is described in detail in the session 11 reading section.

In session 11, the clinician should also tell the student that, starting next week with session 12, meetings will be one time per week instead of two times per week. The clinician and student will need to decide what day of the week meetings will be held for the remaining sessions.

HOPS INTERVENTION SESSION 12 INTRODUCING SELF-MANAGEMENT

HOPS INTERVENTION SESSION 12 – PRESESSION READING

The primary goal of session 12 is to introduce the concept of self-management. Starting with session 12, the clinician and student meet one time per week.

Transition to the Maintenance Phase

Now that sessions are one time per week, the clinician should record teacher initials or accurate homework recording (depending on the student's phase) for the entire past week, since the last HOPS session.

The move to one session per week is the second step in systematically removing the role of the clinician and transferring responsibility for managing the HOPS interventions to the student and the student's parents (the first step was the parent meeting). The goal is to gradually and systematically fade the role the clinician plays. This process should ultimately result in a smooth transition to the postintervention period and should aid the student's continued use of the HOPS intervention skills.

The move to one session per week may be difficult for the student. Meeting two times per week keeps the HOPS intervention system front and center, as the next progress check is always at most 2–3 days away. Further, meeting two times per week helps the student actively maintain materials organization; each time the checklist is completed, the student and clinician are fixing problems. The move to one session per week requires the student to maintain the organization systems to a greater extent because clinician monitoring and delivery of rewards are less frequent. Also, when sessions are one time per week, some of the urgency for maintaining the system is lost. For example, the student can choose to let materials build up in the bookbag and binder for an entire week, with the plan that he or she will clean up everything right before the next session. This strategy increases the likelihood that the student will not be fully prepared for the next HOPS session.

Introduction to Self-Management

The clinician should engage the student in a conversation about how to maintain the HOPS intervention system now that meetings with the clinician are once per week. The self-management checklist should be introduced as part of this discussion as a tool that will help with maintenance (see the template on the supplemental CD-ROM). The self-management checklist is basically an abbreviated version of the checklists completed by the clinician each week. The clinician and the student work together to determine which criteria should be listed on the self-management checklist. Typically, areas to emphasize are those in which the student is having difficulty or further improvement could be made. The checklist should have no more than five criteria listed so that it is easy for the student to complete quickly. The checklist is primarily designed to serve as a prompt or reminder. The student simply circles a yes or no, indicating whether or not each criterion on the checklist was met. The next page shows an example of a completed self-management checklist.

The student already has a materials organization plan in place that specifies when and how frequently the student's binder and bookbag will be cleaned up. The self-management checklist will help the student manage the "what will be accomplished" component of the materials organization plan. Specifically, the clinician and the student will incorporate several criteria from the organizational skills checklist into the student's self-management checklist. The student can then evaluate these criteria using the self-management checklist after completing the clean-up. This will ensure that the student's clean-up was effective. As shown in the example below, the self-management checklist can also be used to help the student remember to use time management skills, such as recording tests and quizzes in the planner.

Examples of Criteria That Could Be Included on the Self-Management Checklist

1. No loose papers are in bookbag.
2. No loose papers are in binder.
3. Homework is recorded accurately and in sufficient detail.
4. Homework to be completed is in the left side of homework folder.

SUPPLEMENT. Example of a completed Self-Management Checklist.

SELF-MANAGEMENT CHECKLIST

Criteria	Dates of Checklist Completion					
	12/2	12/6				
There are no loose papers in my bookbag.	(YES)/NO	(YES)/NO	YES/NO	YES/NO	YES/NO	YES/NO
There are no loose papers in my binder.	YES/(NO)	YES/(NO)	YES/NO	YES/NO	YES/NO	YES/NO
Homework to be completed is in the left side of my homework folder.	(YES)/NO	(YES)/NO	YES/NO	YES/NO	YES/NO	YES/NO
Homework to be turned in is in the right side of my homework folder.	(YES)/NO	(YES)/NO	YES/NO	YES/NO	YES/NO	YES/NO
Steps for planning and studying for tests are recorded in my planner.	YES/(NO)	(YES)/NO	YES/NO	YES/NO	YES/NO	YES/NO

 Supplemental Materials: Blank copies of the forms and letters are provided on the CD. Permission is given for individual teachers, administrators, or other school personnel to reproduce any form labeled "Supplement."

5. Homework to be turned in is in the right side of the homework folder.
6. Steps for test planning and studying are recorded in the planner.
7. All old (not needed) papers and worksheets are thrown away.
8. All papers are in the appropriate class section of the binder.
9. No loose papers are in the locker.

HOPS INTERVENTION SESSION 12 – SESSION CONTENT

Activities to Be Completed

1. Complete the organizational skills checklist and record points.
2. Complete the teacher initials checklist and record points.
3. Complete the time management checklist and record points.
4. Introduce the self-management checklist.

Introducing Self-Management

The clinician should engage the student in a conversation about how to maintain consistent use of the HOPS skills now that meetings with the clinician are once per week.

You have done a really nice job improving your organization, homework, and time management skills. The ultimate goal is for you to manage your materials and homework on your own, without my help, and for your mom or dad to reward your progress. You are already pretty consistent with your performance from week to week, so at this point we are going to move to meeting once per week. How does that sound?

Now that we are meeting once per week instead of twice per week, it may get harder for you to keep up your organization systems and to remember to record homework and tests in your planner. I will be checking less frequently and it will be up to you to remember to keep recording your homework accurately and to keep your bookbag, binder, and locker organized. Let's talk about some strategies you can use to keep your materials organized and homework recorded consistently so that you can keep earning points.

Describing the Self-Management Checklist

After providing the rationale for self-management, the clinician should introduce the checklist as a tool for facilitating the process.

To help you keep earning points, I am going to give you your own checklist, called a self-management checklist. It is much shorter and simpler than the checklists we complete when we meet. You will pick a time each week to evaluate yourself by completing the self-management checklist. Here is an example of a self-management checklist using five criteria. All you do is record the date you completed the checklist and record yes or no to indicate whether you met each criterion. In this example, for the criterion "There are no loose papers in my bookbag," the "yes" has been circled. This means that the student did not have any loose papers in his or her backpack on 12/2 and 12/6. Do you have any questions?

Now let's create a self-management checklist for you. I would like you to help decide what criteria to put on your checklist. We don't want to list more than five criteria. That way it will be easy for you to complete the checklist quickly. We could even start with listing only two or three things if you want. We want to choose the criteria that

SUPPLEMENT. Example of a completed Self-Management Checklist.

SELF-MANAGEMENT CHECKLIST

Criteria	Dates of Checklist Completion					
	12/2	12/6				
There are no loose papers in my bookbag.	(YES)/NO	(YES)/NO	YES/NO	YES/NO	YES/NO	YES/NO
There are no loose papers in my binder.	YES/(NO)	YES/(NO)	YES/NO	YES/NO	YES/NO	YES/NO
Homework to be completed is in the left side of my homework folder.	(YES)/NO	(YES)/NO	YES/NO	YES/NO	YES/NO	YES/NO
Homework to be turned in is in the right side of my homework folder.	(YES)/NO	(YES)/NO	YES/NO	YES/NO	YES/NO	YES/NO
Steps for planning and studying for tests are recorded in my planner.	YES/(NO)	(YES)/NO	YES/NO	YES/NO	YES/NO	YES/NO
	YES/NO	YES/NO	YES/NO	YES/NO	YES/NO	YES/NO
	YES/NO	YES/NO	YES/NO	YES/NO	YES/NO	YES/NO

Supplemental Materials: Blank copies of the forms and letters are provided on the CD. Permission is given for individual teachers, administrators, or other school personnel to reproduce any form labeled "Supplement."

you see as most important in helping you use organization and time management skills consistently. Here are the three checklists that I complete each week. Let's look at these checklists and pick out the most important criteria to record on your self-management checklist.

Creating a Self-Management Plan

Once the self-management checklist is created, the clinician will begin to discuss creating a self-management plan (see the template on the supplemental CD-ROM and the example on the next page) to go along with the checklist. The clinician and student should work together in session to complete the self-management plan. An example script for creating a self-management plan is provided below.

Now that we have created your self-management checklist, we should establish a plan for when you will complete the checklist. How often do you think you should complete the checklist? [The student should complete checklist at least one time per week outside of HOPS sessions.] Is there a certain time that you think it would be easiest for you to go through and complete your checklist? For example, would before school, during school, or after school work best for you? One possibility to consider is that you could complete your self-management checklist right after you finish your organization clean-up each week. Completing the checklist then would help you make sure that you did a good job with the organization clean-up. What do you think?

Great. Let's write all of this information down. We will call this your self-management plan and we can revise and improve your plan if we need to later on. Can you think of a benefit of completing the self-management checklist each week before we meet? That's right. You will earn lots more points because you will come to our meeting fully prepared. I know this might be hard to remember to complete each week. What would be a good reward for you if you came to our next session with the self-management checklist completed?

HOPS INTERVENTION SESSION 13
EXPANDING THE HOME-BASED SYSTEM

HOPS INTERVENTION SESSION 13 – PRESESSION READING

The primary goals of session 13 are to review the student's completion of the self-management checklist and plan and to prepare for the second and final parent meeting.

Review of the Self-Management Checklist

The clinician should check with the student about whether or not he or she was able to complete the self-management checklist during the past week. The clinician can praise the student for completing it or encourage the student to complete it next week if he or she forgot. The majority of time in session 13 will be spent planning for the parent meeting. During session 14, the clinician will have more time to discuss and solve any problems the student had with completing the self-management checklist.

Goals for the Second Parent Meeting

The second and final parent meeting should take place between sessions 13 and 14. The parent meeting has three main goals: (a) to have the student create graphs to show his or her parent the progress that has been

SUPPLEMENT. Self-Management Plan.

SELF-MANAGEMENT PLAN

How often (times per week) will the student complete the checklist?

_____

_____

What day(s)/time(s) will the checklist be completed each week?

_____

_____

Where will the checklist completion take place?

_____

_____

How will the student remember to complete the checklist?

_____

_____

_____

 Supplemental Materials: Blank copies of the forms and letters are provided on the CD. Permission is given for individual teachers, administrators, or other school personnel to reproduce any form labeled "Supplement."

made, (b) to review parent implementation of the missing assignments tracking plan, and (c) to transfer additional monitoring and rewards responsibilities from the clinician to the parent.

Goal 1: Demonstrate the Student's Progress With Graphs

Graphs can be a great way for a student to visually demonstrate his or her progress with the intervention. Some ideas for graphs are provided below.

Graph the student's progress in collecting teacher initials. An example teacher initials graph is provided in Figure 2. This type of graph can be created using graph paper and a ruler or using spreadsheet graphing software on the computer. The number of teacher initials a student could receive each school day should be plotted on the left vertical axis. For example, if 4 is the maximum number of initials a student is expected to receive, the scale would be 0–4 on the left-hand side of the figure. Across the bottom, the clinician should list all school days starting with 1 week before the HOPS intervention (baseline) up to the current HOPS session. If the graph would have to show too many days (i.e., there would be too many points on the graph), the clinician could consider graphing just baseline and the past month of school days. The clinician and student should then be able to fill in the points on the graph using the teacher initials checklist. The student would record a point (dot) for the number of initials received each school day and then use a ruler to connect the dots.

Graph the student's materials organization progress. The clinician may wish to have the student graph three separate lines for each area of organization (i.e., binder, bookbag, and locker, such as in Figure 3) or may wish to have one line highlighting the area in which the student has had the most success. If the clinician wants to graph all three aspects on one graph, a percentage from 0 to 100 should be listed on the vertical axis. The percentage is the number of organization criteria met divided by the total criteria available. For example, if a

FIGURE 2. Graph of teacher initials collected in October.

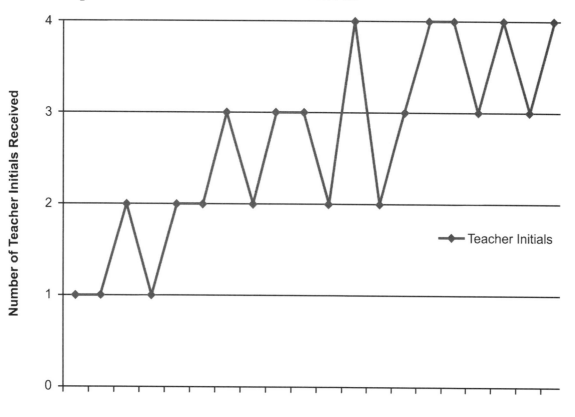

Number of School Days Since Initials Intervention Started

FIGURE 3. Materials organization.

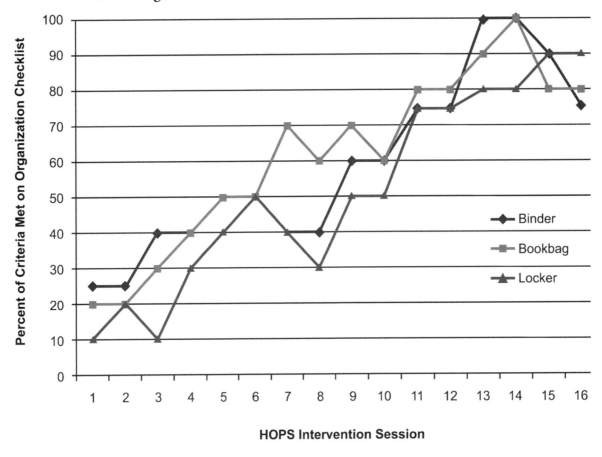

HOPS Intervention Session

student met 5 out of the 7 binder organization criteria, the percentage would 71%. If the clinician chooses to graph only one particular aspect of the HOPS system, such as binder organization, then percentages are not needed, and the number of criteria can be listed on the vertical axis. For example, for binder the range would be 0–7. HOPS session dates would be listed across the bottom showing each time the organization checklist was completed.

Goal 2: Review the Missing Assignments Tracking Plan

During the first parent meeting, the clinician encouraged the parent to review the student's planner every day after school to check for missing assignments. The clinician helped the parent establish a system for rewarding the student's assignment completion. One of the primary goals of this second parent meeting is to review with the parent and student how the home-based system of recording missing assignments is working. In preparation for this, the clinician should spend some time during session 13 discussing the missing assignments system with the student. It is important for the clinician to obtain the student's perspective on how the system is working before bringing it up with the parent. For example, the clinician will want to get an idea of how frequently the parent checks the planner and how consistently rewards or consequences are being implemented.

Goal 3: Transfer Additional Monitoring and Rewards Responsibilities to the Parent

The third goal of the parent meeting is to transfer additional monitoring and reward responsibilities from the clinician to the parent. Specifically, the parent will be asked to maintain the home-based system of tracking missing assignments and also monitor additional HOPS skills (e.g., materials organization).

Additions to the Home-Based Plan

At this point, the parent should already be checking the student's planner for missing assignments and providing rewards or consequences. The other HOPS checklists—organizational skills and time management checklists—are too long and cumbersome for parents to complete regularly. The best option is to provide the parent with a modified version of the student's self-management checklist. This checklist, called the parent checklist (see parent meeting content and the supplemental CD-ROM), can be longer than the student's but should contain no more than 10 criteria for the parent to monitor and reward.

During session 13, the clinician should work with the student to pick criteria to go on the parent checklist and to tentatively discuss the rewards and consequences that will be associated with the parent's completion of the checklist. Working with the student on this plan before the parent meeting will save time during the parent meeting, increase the student's participation in the system, and increase the likelihood that the student will be satisfied with the system of rewards or consequences established during the parent meeting.

Aspects of the Home-Based Plan to Discuss With the Student

The following questions can be used in a discussion of the parent checklist:

What criteria should be listed on the parent checklist? How often will the parent complete the checklist? The clinician and the student currently complete the checklists once per week. If the student's performance has dropped during the maintenance phase, the parent might want to complete the checklist twice per week. In contrast, if the student's performance has stayed consistent during the maintenance phase, then it may be sufficient for the parent to complete the checklist once per week.

What should the rewards and consequences be? For example, parents might want to make daily free time contingent upon completion of the checklist, or they may want to use material rewards.

HOPS INTERVENTION SESSION 13 – SESSION CONTENT

Activities to Be Completed

1. Complete the organizational skills checklist and record points.
2. Complete the teacher initials checklist and record points.
3. Complete the time management checklist and record points.
4. Review the self-management checklist.
5. Prepare for the parent meeting.

Presenting Examples for the Graphing Progress

After the checklists are completed, the clinician should talk to the student about the upcoming parent meeting. The clinician should let the student know that one of the goals of the parent meeting is for the student to show his or her parents how much progress has been made. The clinician can then recommend that the student graph progress in one or two areas to show the parent (see Figures 4 and 5). The clinician can use the following scripts to get started.

FIGURE 4. Graph of teacher initials collected in October.

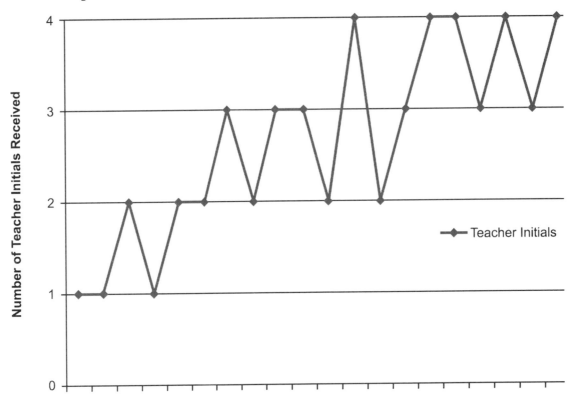

Number of School Days Since Initials Intervention Started

You have really made some nice improvements with your materials organization and homework management. I want to make sure that you have the opportunity to show your [mom/dad] how well you are doing. I think it would be nice if we graphed your progress so that your parents can see a picture of your improvements. One graph we could make would be to chart your progress with obtaining teacher initials. Here is an example of what we could do. This graph shows the number of teacher initials the student received during the month of October. You can see how this student really improved with teacher initials during October. On this graph, a score of 4 is the best because it means that the student received all four core teachers' initials. If you like this idea, we will make a graph like this one charting the improvements you have made with teacher initials.

Here is an example of another graph we could make today [show the student Figure 5]. This graph shows how you are doing with binder, bookbag, and locker organization. We would use the organizational skills checklist to make a graph like this for you. As you can see, across the bottom, meeting dates are listed and the percentage of organization criteria met is listed on the vertical axis. Notice how the three separate lines each track something different. This line tracks the binder, this line tracks the bookbag, and this line tracks the locker. We could graph how you are doing in all three areas or we could just pick one area to graph. What would you like to show your parents?

After the clinician and student have made at least one graph, the clinician should engage the student in a discussion about the other two goals for the parent meeting: (a) to review the home-based missing assignments tracking plan and (b) to transfer additional monitoring and reward responsibilities to the parent.

FIGURE 5. Materials organization progress.

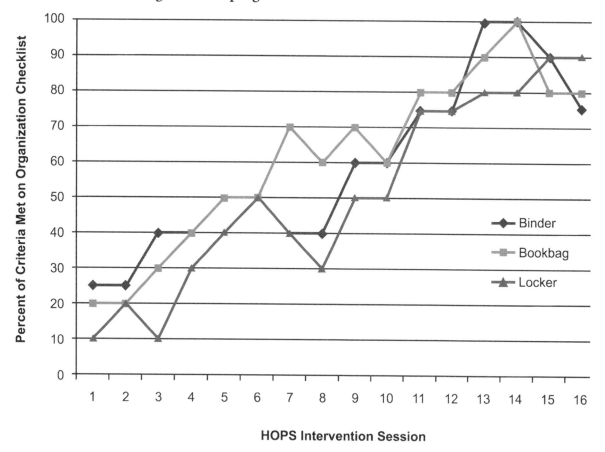

Reviewing the Missing Assignments Home-Based Plan

The clinician should ask the student how the home-based missing assignments tracking plan is going. Getting this information now will give the clinician an idea of how much time may need to be spent revising the plan during the parent meeting. The clinician should ask the student how frequently the parent is checking the planner and how consistently the parent is administering rewards. The clinician should also ask the student how the plan is working and about any ideas for modifications.

After the clinician and student discuss progress with the missing assignments tracking plan, the remainder of the session should be focused on deciding criteria to include on the parent checklist and discussing rewards that the student could earn for meeting the criteria.

Transferring Rewards and Monitoring to the Parent

The clinician can use the following script to explain how the student's parents will take over the role of providing rewards once the HOPS intervention is completed.

When we meet with your [mom/dad], we are going to encourage them to monitor your use of organization and time management skills at home and to reward you for your progress. Your [mom/dad] can monitor your HOPS skills using a short version of the checklists we complete together. This is a great thing for you, because you will still get points from me and you will also have a chance to earn points and rewards at home. However, the checklists we use each week are long and take a lot of time to complete. Let's work together this session to develop a simpler checklist that your [mom/dad] can use to help you stay organized and to track the points that you earn. Let's use your self-management checklist as a model. Here is an example of a checklist that your [mom/dad] could complete each week [see next page]. Let's look at this example and then think about what criteria you think should be on your parents' checklist.

Let's write in criteria that you would like your parents to check on this checklist [see the supplemental CD-ROM for the blank parent checklist form]. *We can present this to your [mom/dad] during the parent meeting and see what they think.*

Establishing Home-Based Rewards

During parent meeting 2, the clinician will help the parent establish a home-based rewards menu similar to the rewards menu the clinician has been using. Specifically, the menu will list a number of different reward options, and each option will have a point value associated with it. Developing the reward menu during the parent meeting will go more smoothly if the clinician and student spend time during session 13 brainstorming possible rewards. The rewards can be material rewards (e.g., a CD or a video game) or they can be privilege-based rewards (e.g., 1 hour extra video game time or 1-hour later bedtime). If a home-based rewards menu is established now, the main task to be accomplished with the parent will be assigning point values to each reward option on the menu. A blank rewards menu is provided on the supplemental CD-ROM for the clinician and student to record ideas. It is important that the clinician help the student be creative in listing rewards. The more reward options there are on the menu, the more meaningful it will be for the student. Students tend to think of material rewards first (e.g., a CD). The clinician should help the student think of nonmaterial reward options. For example, the student may get to choose what the family has for dinner or may get to choose where the family goes to eat out one night per week. The student could also earn "get out of chore" passes or passes to spend time alone with mom or dad, without siblings.

PARENT MEETING 2

HOPS INTERVENTION PARENT MEETING 2

Activities to Be Completed

1. Have the student present the organization and teacher initials graphs to the parent.
2. Review the status of the home-based missing assignments tracking system and make modifications if necessary.
3. Establish a home-based parent checklist monitoring system. Establish criteria to be listed on the parent checklist. Establish a home-based rewards menu.

The primary goal of the second parent meeting is to have the parent leave with a specific plan for completing the parent checklist and assigning rewards and consequences.

The parent checklist is designed to be a streamlined version of the clinician-completed organization and time management checklists. The clinician has been completing these checklists weekly and assigning points. The student has been using the points to earn rewards from a rewards menu. To smooth the transition from clinician tracking to parent tracking, we recommend that the home-based parent system be as similar as possible to the system used by the clinician. Specifically, we recommend that the student earn points at home

SUPPLEMENT. Example of a completed Parent Checklist.

PARENT CHECKLIST

Criteria	Record Dates of Checklist Completion					
There are no loose papers in the binder.	YES/NO	YES/NO	YES/NO	YES/NO	YES/NO	YES/NO
There are no loose papers in the bookbag.	YES/NO	YES/NO	YES/NO	YES/NO	YES/NO	YES/NO
Homework to be completed is in the left side of the homework folder.	YES/NO	YES/NO	YES/NO	YES/NO	YES/NO	YES/NO
Homework to be turned in is in the right side of the homework folder.	YES/NO	YES/NO	YES/NO	YES/NO	YES/NO	YES/NO
Steps for planning and studying for tests are recorded in the planner.	YES/NO	YES/NO	YES/NO	YES/NO	YES/NO	YES/NO
	YES/NO	YES/NO	YES/NO	YES/NO	YES/NO	YES/NO
	YES/NO	YES/NO	YES/NO	YES/NO	YES/NO	YES/NO

 Supplemental Materials: Blank copies of the forms and letters are provided on the CD. Permission is given for individual teachers, administrators, or other school personnel to reproduce any form labeled "Supplement."

for criteria met on the parent checklist and that points go toward rewards on a rewards menu. The student is already used to this type of system, and the adjustment to parent tracking should feel less abrupt this way. Accordingly, one of the main goals of the second parent meeting is for the clinician to help the parent develop a home-based rewards menu.

Guiding Principles for the Parent Checklist and Rewards Plan

A few key components of successful home-based plans are listed below. The clinician probably will not have time to cover each of these principles with the parent during the second meeting. We present these principles here primarily for the clinician to keep in mind in case they come up when discussing how the missing assignments tracking and home-based rewards system are going.

1. The parent should not take away a reward or refuse to give the student a reward that has been earned because of a separate instance of negative behavior. For example, the student had no missing assignments and earned 1 hour of free time. However, the student yelled at a sibling and the parent decided not to give the student free time. It should be explained to the parent that when this happens the student's motivation for the system will decrease quickly. It will seem that it doesn't matter if the student tries with the organization system because "I will just lose the reward anyway" or "Mom will just find some other reason to take it away." It is important that the parent have backup consequences in mind. For example, the parent could take away a privilege for the yelling behavior (e.g., TV), but taking away an earned reward (free time) should not be used as a consequence.

Similarly, the parent should be advised *not* to make too many additional positive behaviors contribute toward earning free time or points. For example, the parent may want to start awarding points for completion of chores or for getting ready for school on time. When too many behaviors are earning points, the system becomes more difficult to implement consistently. Further, the student can stop trying in one area (e.g., organization) and still earn points because of multiple opportunities with other areas (e.g., completion of chores).

2. It is important that the parents agree to a system that they will be able to implement. The clinician should emphasize feasibility when working with the parent to develop a home-based system. One important aspect the clinician needs to emphasize to the parent is the principal of consistency. Home-based systems are rarely successful when the parent does not monitor and reward consistently. Missing the scheduled completion of the checklist may cause the student to believe that (a) the parent doesn't really care about the organization system (i.e., it must not be that important); and (b) the parent is not going to check regularly, so I can get away with not organizing materials regularly. For this reason, we recommend that the parent commit to completing the parent checklist only once or at most two times per week. It would be difficult for most parents to consistently complete the checklist more frequently.

3. It is important that parents have some idea of how to fade out the system over time and that they know that they won't have to check and monitor forever. The clinician should talk to the parent about the principal of "freedom through responsibility." Specifically, once the student shows responsibility for a certain behavior, for example, being organized, then the parent will provide more freedom by doing less monitoring. In fact, reducing the frequency of monitoring can serve as a powerful reward.

The clinician should provide the parent with the example of the two phases of the homework management system. Specifically, when the student demonstrates responsibility (i.e., 75% or better with teacher initials for 2 weeks), additional freedoms are earned (i.e., the student no longer has to obtain teacher initials).

The parent can set specific "responsibility goals" and be clear about what freedoms the student will earn for accomplishing the goals. The clinician may give the parent some specific examples of how the freedom through responsibility principle can be applied at home. For example, the parent could move from completing the parent checklist once per week to once every other week if the student met 90% of the criteria for 2 consecutive weeks.

Demonstrating the Student's Progress

The clinician should begin the meeting by asking the student to present the graphs showing his or her progress. The clinician should have the student tell the parent what specific areas he or she has been working on since the last meeting. The student should be prompted to list all additions to the HOPS intervention system. For example, the parent is probably not aware that the student has a specific materials organization plan that is implemented each week. The clinician should have the student explain the self-management clean-up process and how the new self-management checklist fits into this process. The clinician should also encourage the student to tell the parent about planning for tests, quizzes, and projects and the time management checklist. Time management skills were introduced after the first parent meeting, and the parent probably does not know about this aspect of the HOPS intervention.

Reviewing Progress With the Home-Based Missing Assignments Tracking System

The clinician should start by taking out a copy of the missing assignments tracking plan, completed during the first HOPS parent meeting. *"Last time we met, we created a plan for tracking [student's name's] missing assignments and rewarding completion of assignments. Can you tell me how that is going?"* If the parent answers generally, such as "good," the clinician should ask questions to elicit specific details. *"About how many days per week are you checking [student's name's] planner for missing assignments? How is the reward/consequence plan working? Are you able to consistently follow the plan?"* The clinician can then ask the parent to briefly describe any barriers or problems that have been encountered with the missing assignments tracking system. The clinician should take notes on any barriers that the parent brings up.

We recommend that the clinician hold off on trying to solve problems with the missing assignments tracking plan until the end of the meeting. The clinician will be encouraging the parent to add to the rewards system using the parent checklist. The parent may want to modify the rewards provided for completing assignments to accommodate the new parent checklist system or may want to combine the two reward systems. For that reason, we recommend that the clinician introduce the parent checklist system and then come back to solving any problems with the missing assignments tracking and rewards system.

Introducing the Parent Checklist

The following script can be used to introduce the idea of having the parent monitor the student's progress with the HOPS skills using the parent checklist.

[Student's name] and I spent our last meeting brainstorming ways to ensure that [he/she] maintains all of the gains made with the HOPS program after we stop working together. We only have three more meetings left after today, and I won't be tracking [student's name's] organization, homework, or time management or providing rewards after that. Our main goal for this meeting is to develop a plan that will allow you to maintain some of the tracking and rewarding that I have been doing so that [student's name] keeps using the skills. We need to make sure that the system we pick for you to use at home is something you are able to implement so that you and [student's name] can follow it consistently. [Student's name] has agreed to present some of our ideas to you.

[Student's name], why don't you show your [mom/dad] the parent checklist and tell them about some of your ideas?

Great! To add a bit to what [student's name] said, I have been tracking [student's name's] organization, time management, and homework management every time we meet using these checklists [show parent the student's folder]. Every time we meet, I record what criteria [student's name] meets and I assign points for meeting the criteria. The parent checklist that [student's name] showed you is a simpler, combination of all of these checklists. We picked what we thought were the most important criteria from each checklist and put it all together. Do you think it would be feasible for you to complete this checklist one or two times per week? Can you think of criteria you would like to add to this checklist or criteria you would like to delete? Great. Let's work on developing a specific rewards menu that can be tied to this checklist. We can also discuss how this checklist fits in with the missing assignments tracking you are already doing.

Developing the Parent Rewards Menu

At this point in the parent meeting, the clinician should have the student present the parent rewards menu developed during the last session. The clinician should solicit the parent's input to determine if the rewards on the menu are acceptable. The clinician can also obtain the parent's input about additional reward options. The clinician, student, and parent can then work to assign point values to each of the rewards.

Assigning Point Values to Rewards

The following script describes to the parent how the rewards menu and points system work.

There are [X] number of criteria on the parent checklist we created, and you are going to complete the checklist [X] times per week. If each criterion on the checklist is worth 1 point, that means that [student's name] can earn a total of [X] points per week. Ideally, we would want [student's name] to be able to earn one reward every week if [he/she] does well with organization and time management. It may take longer for [student's name] to earn some of these bigger rewards, and that is okay. We want [student's name] to have the option of turning in the points each week for a smaller reward or saving points for a bigger reward. Either is fine. Which of the rewards on this menu do you think are okay for [student's name] to earn each week? Okay. That means that each of these rewards should be worth about [X] points. How about we make these bigger rewards worth twice as many points, so [X] points each? Does that sound okay?

Developing the Specific Home-Based Plan

The last step in the process is for the clinician and parent to finalize the specifics of the plan. For example, how frequently and when will the parent checklist be completed? The clinician should also spend some time exploring potential problems and how they could be handled. What if the student doesn't bring home the bookbag and binder to be checked on the appropriate day? What would the parent do? A template for recording the specific details of the home-based plan is provided on the supplemental CD-ROM.

HOPS SESSION 14
TROUBLESHOOTING SELF-MANAGEMENT PLANS

HOPS INTERVENTION SESSION 14 – PRESESSION READING

The primary goals of session 14 are to review and process the parent meeting and to make adjustments to the student's self-management system.

Self-Management Versus Parent Management

The student's self-management checklist and the parent checklist are very similar. It may seem that the student tracking and monitoring system is redundant with the parent system. These two tracking systems purposely overlap to account for the fact that neither system is likely to be implemented with the frequency and consistency that the clinician provided. Ideally, the student would complete the self-management checklist once per week and the parent would complete the parent checklist once or twice per week. If this occurred, a subset of the student's HOPS skills would be monitored and rewarded with a frequency comparable to when the student was working with the clinician. In reality, what often happens is that the student does well maintaining certain aspects of his or her self-management system (e.g., the self-organization clean-up) and the parent does well with certain aspects of the home-based system (e.g., tracking missing assignments). Together, their efforts combine to help the student maintain the use of the new skills over time. In addition, we recommend that HOPS skills tracking and monitoring be incorporated into 504 or IEP plans whenever possible. The goal is to establish multiple systems of monitoring and rewarding that, in combination, will support the student's continued use of HOPS skills.

The parent will now be evaluating the student on organization and time management criteria that overlap with the criteria on the clinician's HOPS checklists. The clinician should continue to complete all of the HOPS checklists separately as part of each session and should continue to provide the student with points for all tasks completed. This continuity is important, because it will take a while for the parent to implement the system consistently and for the student to start building up points toward home-based rewards.

Review of the Parent Meeting

Another important task for the clinician is to spend some time in session 14 processing the parent meeting with the student. The meeting may not have gone exactly as planned, or the parent may not have accepted the rewards system proposed by the student. For these reasons, it is important to determine how the student thinks the meeting went and to give the student the opportunity to vent frustrations. The clinician should ask the student what types of problems, if any, he or she anticipates occurring with the home system. The clinician should let the student know that progress with the home-based system will be reviewed in all HOPS sessions from this point forward. The clinician should emphasize that it is important for the student to be honest about whether or not the home system is working so that the clinician knows if adjustments need to be made.

Review of the Implementation of the Self-Management Plan

The clinician should review the self-management plan and see how the student is performing since moving to the maintenance phase and one session per week. The clinician should consider adding to the graphs created for the parent meeting. This will provide data showing the student's progress since entering the maintenance phase.

The clinician could draw a vertical line on the graph between sessions 11 and 12, indicating where the training phase ended and the maintenance phase began. After reviewing this data, the clinician will have a better idea of how the self-management plan is going and what changes need to be made. In the session content, we describe problems students commonly have with the self-management plan and provide potential solutions.

HOPS INTERVENTION SESSION 14 – SESSION CONTENT

Activities to Be Completed

1. Complete the organizational skills checklist and record points.
2. Complete the teacher initials checklist and record points.
3. Complete the time management checklist and record points.
4. Review the parent meeting.
5. Review implementation of the self-management plan.

Reviewing the Parent Meeting

The clinician can use the following script to discuss the parent meeting and how the home-based monitoring system is working so far.

Last week we met with your [mom/dad] and had a chance to discuss all of the new skills you have learned. You were able to show your [mom/dad] the graphs we made charting your progress, and we talked about starting a home-based system. How do you think the meeting went? How do you feel about the home-based rewards system we discussed in the meeting? [Clinician should take a minute to review the home-based system agreed upon during the parent meeting.] Do you think it will work? How is it going so far? Are there any parts of the home-based system that you think might be difficult or cause problems at home?

From now on when you and I meet, we will discuss how the home-based rewards system is going. If you think there are any aspects of the home-based system that aren't working, let me know, and we can work together to fix the problems. The most important thing is to make sure we create a system that works for you and helps you keep up the great work you have been doing.

Reviewing the Implementation of the Self-Management Plan

The clinician and the student should continue graphing the student's intervention progress. It may be helpful to draw a vertical line on the graph indicating where the training phase stops and the maintenance phase begins. That way the student and clinician can determine if performance has changed as a result of moving to one session per week.

The clinician should ask the student about the self-management plan and whether it was adhered to. The clinician should also ask the student's opinion about whether or not to make changes to the plan. If the student adhered to the plan and showed consistent performance, the first script can be used.

Wow! You are doing a great job staying organized! It looks like your self-management plan is working pretty well for you. How do you think it's been going? Have you been sticking with it? Has it been easy or hard for you to complete the self-management checklist? Are there any changes you would like to make that will help you keep making progress?

If the student's performance dropped between session 11 and session 14, the clinician should ask about the student's adherence to the plan. If the student did not follow through with the planned system, the clinician and student will need to determine if (a) the self-management plan is fine and likely to be effective (i.e., the student just needs more time to get used to the new system), or (b) adjustments or additions need to be made to the student's plan. When necessary, the clinician should help the student make changes to improve the self-management plan.

As you can see from the graphs, your progress decreased slightly since we moved to the self-management plan and meeting once a week. Let's work together to get your performance back up. How has the self-management plan been going for you? Have you been sticking with it? Has it been easy or hard for you to remember to complete the checklist? What changes do you think need to be made to the self-management plan to help you keep making progress?

Evaluating the Self-Management Plan

Below are some factors for the clinician to consider when evaluating the student's self-management plan.

1. Is the self-management plan feasible or too complex? What is feasible will vary from student to student. It is important to determine if the student has aimed too high and has potentially committed to a plan that he or she is not able to follow through with consistently. For example, for some students, the plan of keeping materials organized as needed or constantly is not feasible. At the end of class when the bell rings and the student has 5 minutes to get to the next class, he or she may not have the patience or time needed to file papers in the appropriate section of their binder.

If a student wants to adhere to a system in which he or she remains consistently organized, then the clinician may want to recommend a "to be filed" folder for the binder. This is a folder in which the student can put all loose papers when he or she is in a rush and doesn't have time to file. The student can then pick a time to catch up with materials organization. For example, the student might take papers from the to-be-filed folder and put them in the appropriate binder sections at the end of the school day or on the bus ride home.

If the student has designed a system that is too complex, the clinician should work to systematically reduce extraneous elements of the system. For example, if the student indicated that he or she was going to complete the self-organization clean-up every day after school and only accomplished the task on 3 days, the clinician might recommend a trial period in which the student commits to completing the clean-up 2 days per week to see if that is sufficient.

2. Is the system not specific enough? The student's self-management plan and system need to be very detailed and specific, similar to how the materials organization plan was developed. For example, for most students, the plan "I will complete the self-management checklist on Wednesdays" will be ineffective. First, it is not clear what completing the checklist means. Will the student just circle yes or no or actually take the time to fix all of the criteria that were not met. Second, stating "on Wednesdays" in general (i.e., no specific time) increases the likelihood that the student will delay completing the checklist until the last possible minute and he or she may forget or run out of time. The clinician should work with the student to establish and document a specific self-management plan. For example, the plan should list exactly when the student plans to complete the checklist and what actions will occur if the checklist criteria are not met. All of the specific components of the plan should be recorded on the self-management plan (see the supplemental CD-ROM).

3. Is the self-management check not frequent enough? Students often receive many new papers and materials during the week, and completing the self-management checklist and reorganization of materials once a week may not be sufficient. Further, doing all of the organization of materials at once (cleaning out the system) may take a long time, be overwhelming, and cause the student to avoid the process. In this case, the clinician should encourage the student to complete multiple, shorter checks during the week. For example, the student could clean up the bookbag on Tuesdays and clean up the binder on Thursdays.

4. Do the targets on the self-management checklist need to be modified? For example, if the targets on the self-management checklist are all specific to materials organization and the student has failed to record and plan for tests during the past 2 weeks, the clinician and student may want to modify the checklist criteria. The student and clinician can add criteria (e.g., record upcoming tests) if the checklist contains fewer than five criteria. If the checklist already contains five criteria, the clinician and student should delete the criterion that seems least relevant. Alternatively, the student may be overwhelmed with the five criteria listed on the self-management checklist. It may be better to revise the checklist to contain only one or two criteria and to make sure the student is successful before adding additional criteria.

HOPS SESSION 15
REVIEWING STUDENT PROGRESS AND PLANNING AHEAD

HOPS INTERVENTION SESSION 15 – PRESESSION READING

The primary goal of session 15 is to talk with the student about the HOPS intervention coming to an end and to review the student's progress.

Review of the Student's Progress and Setting of Realistic Expectations

Sessions 15 and 16 are the last two HOPS intervention sessions, and session 15 is the last session in which the clinician will complete the HOPS checklists. The clinician should engage the student in a conversation about the intervention ending. Even if the student has not particularly enjoyed the HOPS intervention, he or she likely has developed a relationship with the clinician and may have mixed feelings about stopping the HOPS meetings. As part of the termination process, a helpful approach is for the student and clinician to step back and reflect on how the student's work with the HOPS intervention relates to the big picture—that is, the relationship between the student's hard work with the HOPS intervention and his or her academic performance, family functioning, and self-esteem.

The clinician could start the session by having the student review everything that has been accomplished. The clinician can then ask the student to talk about how all of his or her hard work with HOPS might affect academic performance. Similarly, the clinician could prompt the student to discuss how all of the improvements might affect family relationships. During this discussion, the clinician should make the point that the larger objective takes time, such as improving school grades or relationships with family members. For example, we would not expect a student to show dramatic improvements in school grades immediately following completion of the HOPS intervention. The student will continue to perfect the HOPS skills and to implement them more efficiently and effectively. The clinician can help the student realize that seeing the full benefits of the student's hard work will take time. The goal of this discussion is to reinforce as strongly as possible that the end of the HOPS intervention is only the end of working with the clinician and should not viewed as the end of making improvements with organization, homework, and time management.

The clinician is encouraged to discuss termination of the HOPS intervention as a beginning rather than as an end. Specifically, the purpose of the HOPS intervention was to give the student and student's parents the skills that they needed to continue to make improvements on their own. Students' hard work with the HOPS intervention gets them ready to begin managing their own materials and homework with some parental support. In other words, because the student has worked hard, he or she no longer needs the clinician's support to succeed. In session 15, the clinician and student should take time to celebrate this fact. The clinician should also challenge the student to continue to maintain and perfect the HOPS skills. The clinician should consider offering to touch base with the student in the future if the student wants advice on making changes to the self-management system.

HOPS INTERVENTION SESSION 15 – SESSION CONTENT

Activities to Be Completed

1. Complete the organizational skills checklist and record points.
2. Complete the teacher initials checklist and record points.
3. Complete the time management checklist and record points.
4. Review the student's progress with the HOPS intervention and discuss termination.

Reviewing Progress and Discussing Termination

The final script gathers input from the student about the program and asks him or her to consider how to maintain use of the HOPS skills after the intervention ends.

Today is the last time I will complete the HOPS checklists. Next time we meet is our last HOPS meeting, and I want to spend all of that meeting celebrating your accomplishments. You can turn in any points you have left now or during our next meeting.

I wanted to spend some time today getting your input on how you think the HOPS program has gone for you. Getting your opinions about the HOPS program will help me when I work with other students. What aspects of the HOPS program did you like the best? In what areas do you think you have improved? What areas do you think you need to keep working on? How confident are you that you will be able to continue using the HOPS skills? What skills were the hardest for you to learn? Do you think I should spend more time teaching those skills in the future?

I want to encourage you to think about the end of the HOPS intervention as the beginning of your improvements with organization and homework management, not the end of your improvements. The whole goal of the HOPS program was to get you to a place where you could maintain your organization and homework management systems on your own, without my help. You are definitely there now. That doesn't mean that you will be able to stop working hard though. In fact, the opposite is true. In my experience, students actually make the most gains in terms of improving school grades after they stop working with me. That is because they keep working hard and making adjustments to their systems to make them better. Students get better and better at these skills over time, and as a result they start to see improvements in other areas, such as grades in school. That is why I said that the end of the HOPS intervention is actually the beginning. This is when you take charge of your organization and homework management.

HOPS SESSION 16
CELEBRATING STUDENT PROGRESS

HOPS INTERVENTION SESSION 16 – SESSION CONTENT

The primary goal of session 16 is to celebrate the student's progress with the intervention. The clinician does not need to complete any of the HOPS checklists during session 16. The clinician should have the student cash in all remaining HOPS points for rewards. The session should be spent completing a fun activity, such as playing a board game or a game on the computer.

Chapter 4

Beyond the HOPS Intervention—Choosing the Next Steps

Congratulations on completing the HOPS intervention. This is a good time to step back and to evaluate the student's progress with materials organization and homework completion. At this point, the student should be consistently completing and turning in his or her homework assignments. If this is not the case, the clinician should evaluate where in the homework completion cycle things are breaking down. The homework completion cycle can be divided into four components: (a) recording homework accurately and consistently, (b) bringing the necessary materials home, (c) getting homework completed at home, and (d) bringing materials back to school and turning assignments in to the teacher. Students who have participated in the HOPS intervention are typically completing most of these activities well, but they may continue to have difficulties with one or two specific components. After working with the student for the past 11 weeks, the clinician may be able to pinpoint the specific area of difficulty and make recommendations for additional intervention or follow-up. For example, it might be evident from the parent meetings that the student and parent are fighting about homework each day after school and homework is not getting completed. The clinician might recommend that the parent attend a parent training course or work with a therapist to learn strategies for dealing with noncompliant behaviors.

This is also a good time to assess where the student is with their overall school functioning. For some students, the HOPS intervention alone will be sufficient for getting them to perform at their full academic potential. For other students, additional intervention will be required. If the student is now turning in homework consistently and planning adequately for tests but continues to have poor school grades, additional assessment is necessary. In cases in which the student is planning and preparing adequately but performing poorly on tests and quizzes, evaluation for a learning disorder may be warranted. Alternatively, the student may be receiving poor grades because of his or her own behavioral difficulties at school. If the HOPS rewards system was successful at improving the student's materials organization, the system may also be effective as applied to the student's behavior in the classroom. The clinician may be able to transfer the HOPS points system from academic to behavioral targets. Specifically, the student could earn points in the classroom for appropriate behaviors, such as staying on-task and participating in class. In our experience, the transition to a behavioral points system goes smoothly because the student is already used to, and motivated by, the points system.

Even if no additional intervention is required, the clinician should implement a plan to follow up with the student's materials organization and homework management skills later in the school year. In some of our earlier research, we found that students benefited from a booster session a few months after completing the HOPS intervention. During the booster session, the clinician reviewed the student's planner and completed the organizational skills checklist. The remainder of the session was spent identifying and solving problems and making adjustments to the student's system. Often, students' systems only require minor adjustments to get them back on track. Over time, students tend to revert to relying on memory and may stop recording homework assignments consistently or in enough detail. With a bit of encouragement from the clinician, students will typically get back on track using the skills that they learned with the HOPS intervention.

References

Abikoff, H., & Gallagher, R. (2008a). Assessment and remediation of organizational skills deficits in children with ADHD. In K. McBurnett, L. Pfiffner, G. Elliott, R. Schachar, & J. Nigg (Eds.), *Attention Deficit/ Hyperactivity Disorder: 21st century perspective* (pp. 137–152). New York: Marcel Dekker.

Abikoff, H., & Gallagher, R. (2008b). *Children's organizational skills scales: Technical manual.* North Tonawanda, NY: Multi-Health Systems, Inc.

Atkins, M. S., Pelham, W. E., & Licht, M. H. (1989). The differential validity of teacher ratings of inattention/ overactivity and aggression. *Journal of Abnormal Child Psychology, 17*(4), 423–435.

American Psychiatric Association. (2000). *Diagnostic and statistical manual of mental disorders* (4th ed.). Washington, DC: Author.

Barkley, R. A. (2006). Attention-deficit/hyperactivity disorder: A handbook for diagnosis and treatment (3rd ed.). New York: Guilford Press.

Barkley, R. A., Murphy, K. R., & Fischer, M. (2008). *ADHD in adults: What the science tells us.* New York: Guilford Press.

Blase, S. L., Gilbert, A. N., Anastopoulos, A. D., Costello, E. J., Hoyle, R. H., Swartzwelder, H. S., & Rabiner, D. L. (2009). Self-reported ADHD and adjustment in college: Cross-sectional and longitudinal findings. *Journal of Attention Disorders, 13*(3), 297–309.

DuPaul, G. J., & Stoner, G. (2003). *ADHD in the schools: Assessment and intervention strategies* (2nd ed.). New York: Guilford Press.

Epstein, M. H., Polloway, E. A., Foley, R. M., & Patton, J. R. (1993). Homework: A comparison of teachers' and parents' perceptions of the problems experienced by students identified as having behavioral disorders, learning disabilities, or no disabilities. *Remedial and Special Education, 14*, 40–50.

Evans, S. W., Langberg, J. M., & Williams, J. (2003). Treatment generalization in school-based mental health. In M. Weist, S. Evans, & N. Lever (Eds.), *Handbook of school mental health: Advancing practice and research* (pp. 335–348). New York: Kluwer/Plenum.

Evans, S. W., Serpell, Z., Schultz, B. K., & Pastor, D. A. (2007). Cumulative benefits of secondary school-based treatment of students with attention-deficit hyperactivity disorder. *School Psychology Review, 36*, 256–273.

Frazier, T. W., Youngstrom, E. A., Glutting, J. J., & Watkins, M. W. (2007). ADHD and achievement: Meta-analysis of the child, adolescent, and adult literatures and a concomitant study with college students. *Journal of Learning Disabilities, 40*(1), 49–65.

Froehlich, T. E., Lanphear, B. P., Epstein, J. N., Barberesi, W. J., Katusic, S. K., & Kahn, R. S. (2007). Prevalence and treatment of Attention-Deficit/Hyperactivity Disorder in a national sample of U.S. children. *Archives of Pediatrics and Adolescent Medicine, 161*(9), 857–864.

Knoff, H. M. (2009). Implementing response-to-intervention at the school, district, and state levels: Functional assessment, data-based problem solving, and evidenced-based academic and behavioral interventions. Little Rock, AR: Project ACHIEVE Press.

Langberg, J. M., Arnold, L. E., Flowers, A. M., Altaye, M., Epstein, J. N., & Molina, B. S. G. (2010). Assessing homework problems in children with ADHD: Validation of a parent-report measure and evaluation of homework performance patterns. *School Mental Health, 2*(1), 3–12.

Langberg, J. M., Culp, H., Epstein, J. N., Rockwell, L., & Vaughn, A. J. (2010, June). Development of a school-based organizational skills intervention to improve the academic achievement of adolescents with ADHD. Poster presented at the annual Institute for Education Sciences (IES) research conference, National Harbor, MD.

Langberg, J. M., Epstein, J. N., Altaye, M., Molina, B. S. G., Arnold, L. E., & Vitiello, B. (2008). The transition to middle school is associated with changes in the developmental trajectory of ADHD symptomatology in young adolescents with ADHD. *Journal of Clinical Child and Adolescent Psychology, 37*(3), 651–663.

Langberg, J. M., Epstein, J. N., & Graham, A. (2008). The use of organizational skills interventions in the treatment of children, adolescents and adults with ADHD. *Expert Review of Neurotherapeutics, 8*(10), 1549–1561.

Langberg, J. M., Epstein, J. N., Urbanowicz, C., Simon, J., & Graham, A. (2008). Efficacy of an organization skills intervention to improve the academic functioning of students with ADHD. *School Psychology Quarterly, 23*(3), 407–417.

Langberg, J. M., Smith, B. H., Bogle, K. E., Schmidt, J. D., Cole, W. R., & Pender, C. (2006). A pilot evaluation of Small Group Challenging Horizons Program: A randomized trial. *Journal of Applied School Psychology, 23*(1), 31–58.

Molina, B. S. G., Hinshaw, S. P., Swanson, J. M., Arnold, L. E., Vitiello, B., Jensen, P. S., & the MTA Cooperative Group. (2009). The MTA at 8 years: Prospective follow-up of children treated for combined type ADHD in a multisite study. *Journal of the American Academy of Child and Adolescent Psychiatry, 48*(5), 484–500.

Norwalk, K., Norvilits, J. M., & MacLean, M. G. (2009). ADHD symptomatology and its relationship to factors associated with college adjustment. *Journal of Attention Disorders, 13*(3), 251–258.

Pfiffner, L. J., Mikami, A. Y., Huang-Pollock, C., Easterlin, B., Zalecki, C., & McBurrnet, K. (2007). A randomized, controlled trial of integrated home-school behavioral treatment for ADHD, Predominately Inattentive Type. *Journal of the American Academy of Child and Adolescent Psychiatry, 46*(8), 1041–1050.

Power, T. J., Karustis, J. L., & Habboushe, D. F. (2001). *Homework success for children with ADHD: A family-school intervention program.* New York: Guilford Press.

Power, T. J., Werba, B. E., Watkins, M. W., Angelucci, J. G., & Eiraldi, R. B. (2006). Patterns of parent-reported homework problems among adhd-referred and non-referred children. *School Psychology Quarterly, 21*, 13–33.

Reaser, A., Prevatt, F., Petscher, Y., & Proctor, B. (2007). The learning and study strategies of college students with ADHD. *Psychology in the Schools, 44*(6), 627–638.

Safren, S. A., Otto, M. W., Sprich, S., Winett, C. L., Wilens, T. E., & Biederman, J. (2005). Cognitive-behavioral therapy for ADHD in medication-treated adults with continued symptoms. *Behaviour Research and Therapy, 43*, 831–842.

Zentall, S. S., Harper, G. W., & Stormont-Spurgin, M. (1993). Children with hyperactivity and their organizational abilities. *Journal of Educational Research, 87*(2), 112–117.

Index